DEPARTMENT OF JUSTICE

Slavery, Involuntary Servitude & Peonage

ANTOINETTE HARRELL

Contents

FORWARD

I am honored to be associated with Antoinette Harrell, who runs a nonprofit organization in New Orleans known as "Gathering of Hearts." She has researched files on 20th Century slavery in the states courthouses and the National Archives. This enhanced her work as an activist, finding individual families and communities in the Black Belt who has links to the story of 20th Century slavery, and helping those who desperately need food, clothing and shelter. As a result, she had become the lifeline to many isolated communities, ferrying clothing and food into Louisiana and the Mississippi Delta to poor Black people, Native Americans and others. In late February of 2009, she and Ines Soto arranged a poverty tour the Mississippi Delta. She and her associate Walter Black, Sr., lead and I agreed to accompany them inasmuch as it would give me a 21st century opportunity to see my with my own eyes what my research on the documents had revealed—the damaging results of slavery at the close of the 20th century and it extension into the civil right period.

On February 22, 2009 as Mardi Gras weekend began,

three vans of travelers and a U-Haul truck holding full of clothing left New Orleans, taking Route 55 out of Louisiana beginning the " Those Left Behind" Poverty Tour." Our delegation, which constituted a group of college students, professors, journalist and representatives form the Southern Christian Leadership Conference, visited several Mississippi small towns and communities of Black people in places like Marks, Lambert and Glen Allan in Quitman, Coahoma and Washington counties.

There have been largely unproductive efforts that have helped some, but for most they amounted to wasted dreams. Even where there has been appeared to be some recognition of the scope of the problem, the frame of reference had been problematic as well. It is clear that the "zone" and "new market" approaches of the past that depended on tax incentive investments to lure companies into the region to spur economic growth and increase the accompanying employment have been based on the model of urban poverty. These approaches have not taken into consideration the deep issues embedded in rural Black poverty that stem from the enslavement of the people that were transferred to urban area a few generation ago.

Poverty tours into the Delta are not new; the late Senator from Minnesota, Paul Wellstone and two-time Democratic Presidential candidate, John Edwards made poverty tours in the South. On Edward's poverty tour while running for president in 2008, he came to Quitman County and heard people begging for jobs. Now the difference is that there is a Black President in the White House and he had announced a focus on poverty in his Urban Policy. Those who have been left behind wondered aloud on the tour to what extent President Barrack Obama would find a way around the governors, to direct money into these desperate communities. I wonder, whether the focus on poverty in the White House Office on Urban Policy will only care for those in the metropolitan areas of the country as the plan indicates and not reach out into the people hiding in neglected communities in the Black Belt behind acres and acres of cotton that in many ways is still King in the Delta.

Dr. Ron Walters
Columnist, Political Analyst, a Professor, a Commentator

.... *The Untold Stories In Their Words*

The documents, letters, and reports in this book has no
grammatical corrections are changes.

ACKNOWLEDGMENTS

First I would like to thank my Heavenly Father for inspiring me to conduct and document research on peonage My colleague Walter C. Black, Sr., for scanning thousands of documents at the National Archives and taking photographs for this book. Also thank you for driving me throughout the Mississippi Delta and Louisiana and being one of the supporters who never left my side.

I want to thank my friends Janice and Corretha Israel for all their support and encouragement. Thank you ladies for picking me up at the airport and providing transportation to the National Archives. Film makers Carl Millender, Donald Crenshaw, Glyniss Vernon Gordon, Mayor Johnny Thomas of Glendora, Mississippi, Professor Rebecca Hensley of Southeastern Louisiana University.

Special thanks to the following people, Ines Soto who helped collect clothes, food and other items needed for people in the Mississippi Delta, photographer Shawn Escoffery, my two sons Joseph and Bernard, my beautiful grandchildren Joelle, Chase, Connor, and Carter, Ali Kareem and Tedarrell Muhammad for feeding and clothing the people in the Mississippi Delta, Radio Talk Show Host Bev Smith, Dr. Ron Daniels, Hal Clark-FM-98 Radio, Linda Hill, Rev. John Mosley, Joshua Johnson, and Nathaniel Nasi, who drove truck loads of items to the Mississippi Delta, Adjunct Professor Clare Washington of Portland State University for teaching classes on peonage.

I want to thank Health Care Consultant Avell Stokes, who traveled throughout Palmer Crossing in Forrest County, Mississippi to help those in need. A special thanks to Al White, Mayor Johnny Dupree of Hattiesburg, Mississippi, Mayor Trace Mims of Webb, Mississippi, Photojournalist Wessam Albadry, Photojournalist Kris Davidson, Vera Warren Williams owner of Community Book Store for collecting clothes and books. Bonita Connor, Rev. Dr. Al Sampson. Pastor and Mrs. Junious Buchanan, Sis. Frankie James, Robert Harrell, Sr. for their contributions and donations that helped. My childhood friend Doris Lloyd for pushing me to move forward, and Leonard Smith III, for guiding through the rough roads. My cousin Edwin Temple for all his support. A special thanks to Kaazim Muhammad and his family for helping those in need in Palmer Crossing, Mississippi

Dedication

To the late Mae Louise Wall Miller, the late Dr. Ron Walters, the late Kojo Livingston, the late Cain Wall, Sr., the late Cain Wall, Jr., and the late Ernestine Wall Hill.

To all the African Americans, Hungarians, Polissh, Native Americans, Italians, Mexicans, poor Whites, poor Jews.

......We went back

Prologue

When will slavery end in America? The American history books teach us that enslaved African Americans in the United States of America celebrated their freedom in 1863, when President Abraham Lincoln freed African Americans by enacting the Emancipation Proclamation.

What if slavery continued for African American people in sixteen states and twenty-seven counties throughout Mississippi, from Kosciusko Mississippi the childhood hometown of Oprah Winfrey to the hometown of Morgan Freeman, Clarksdale, Mississippi down to the lonely roads of Money, Mississippi where Emmett Till was murdered in 1955.

What if the same hunger for a slave economy still nourished America's soils and perverted Southern appetite as it feast along the mightiest rivers? Deep in the bowels of America's richest agricultural belt a behind a million cotton bolts. Lived the 20th century masters and Blacks, who were still under the whips and flogging of the master and overseers. Still working from sun up to sun down, who dares to utter the word "slavery," yet lived its reality each and every backbreaking day. So why don't you know anything about slavery in the 20th Century? The U.S. Government knew, the FBI knew, the NAACP knew, Governor Earl Brewer of Mississippi knew, President Calvin Coolidge President Franklin D. Roosevelt knew, local sheriffs elected officials knew, and the Supreme Court knew, you didn't know because the truth of this American nightmare—for those lived it—has been buried in an unnamed darkness in dusty courthouse attics and the National Archives, "Department of Justice files in Washington, D.C."

I have dedicated the last ten years of my life exposing the truth and facts. I researched through thousands of documents housed in the National Archives and traveled throughout Mississippi, searching through criminal and civil documents as it relates to peonage "Involuntary Servitude " a condition of slavery.

Antoinette Harrell conducting peonage
Peonage research at the National Archives College Park, Maryland, NARA
Photo Credit: Walter C. Black, Sr.
RG 60 General Records of the Department of Justice
D.J. Central Files
Classified Subject Files

CHAPTER ONE
ATTORNEY DOCUMENT

ROBERT L. McLENDON
ATTORNEY AT LAW
SEBASTOPOL, MISSISSIPPI

May 4th, 1927

The Department of Justice,

Washington, D.C.

Dear Sirs:

Another nice little case of peonage down here at Sebastopol, in the form of a 16 year old half white negro boy, an orphan, out of Vicksburg, who, seeking employment, chanced to get into Sebastopol some months ago and fell into the hands of Mr. Nick Lang and his boys, W.D. and others. Three times this boy has run away from him, seeking to become free, but is persued and captured and overtaken wherever he may go and taken back upon the farm and put to work. This unfortunate boy tells us that he has been several times beaten by one of the Langs, with his clothes taken off. He gets only his food and clothes and no suit to change in and sleeps in a barn, the cracks of the floor would represent the slatted south end of a chicken house in south Florida as for ventilation. Will Hataway, a "retired capitalist" and "news agent" for his brother-in-law, Lang, only this morning helped catch this 16 year old negro orphan by running him around a house, and when he caught him he told his kinsfolks to tie him and take him back home and whip him. How is this for slavery? I cannot recall the name of the boy but an early trip to Mr. Nick Langs home a mile west of Sebastopol on the Sebastopol and Demascus public road will find the boy in slavery all right. Now, gentlemen, if a man comes down spreading his great mission to the four winds the facts may never be known. If some one will come down and have nothing to say to any one, but only to the little negro boy, and that out in strict privacy, he can get the book full of peonage, slavery and involuntary servitude, violative of all the laws of the United States and Arkansaw, from this single instance, as to whether slavery is still on in the beautiful, intelectual, Christian Southdom. I have no ax to grind. No enemy to persecute. I am just a human. And I believe a negro is a human. And I believe that in 1865 slavery was sent back to hell in the United States from whence it sprang. I believe in the land of the free and home of the brave. But inasmuch as we have but little law enforcement in the right direction in Scott County Mississippi, and most of that persecution law, I hands-oof and pass this up to you. A nest of kinsfolks here will soon let you know that hell is an icehouse when you seek to investigate slavery and moonshining and bootlegging. If we had one Federal officer in this part of Mississippi who himself was sober and honest, a land office business would be done here capturing the bootleggers and moonshiners about Sebastopol also. No State officer will do anything with them in Scott County. We think it not right to advertise our part we play in this matter to the slave-holders, as we dont want to be forced to make a sieve of any one or more of them. The banker here is a kinsman to the nest. If the negro boy is taken and carried off away from them he will relate facts to you that will make you know he is just a plain, open door negro slave, serving his time in bonds to a dominating master.

Yours truly, Robert L. McLendon

And many other slaves over Mississippi, Alabama and Ga., being smuggled.

Robert L. McClendon

Attorney At Law

Sebastopol, Mississippi

May 4, 1925

Department of Justice

Washington, D.C.

Dear Sirs:

Another nice little case of peonage down here at Sebastopol in the form of a 16 year old half white negro boy, an orphan, out of Vicksburg, who seeking employment, chanced to get into Sebastopol some months ago and fell into the hands of Mr. Nick Lang and his boys, W.D. and others. Three times this boys has run away from him, seeking to become free, but is pursued and captured and overtaken wherever he may go and taken back upon the farm and put to work. This unfortunate boy tells us that he has been several times beaten by one of the Lang's, with his clothes taken off. He gets only his food and clothes and no suit to change in and sleeps in a barn, the cracks of the floor would represent the slatted south end of a chicken house in south Florida as for ventilation. Will Hataway, a 'retired capitalist' and 'news agent' for his brother-in-law Lang, only this morning help catch this to year old negro orphan by running him around the house, when he caught him he told his kinsfolk's to tie him and him back home and whip him. How is this for slavery? I cannot recall the name of the boy Sebastopol and Demascus public road will find the boy in slavery all right. Now, Gentlemen, if a man comes done spreading his great mission to the four nothing to say to any one, but only to the little negro boy, and that out in strict privacy, he can get the book full of peonage, slavery and involuntary violation of all the laws of the United States and Arkansaw from electoral, Christian Southdom. I have to ax to grind. No enemy to persecute. I am just a human. And I believe a Negro is a human. And I believe that in 1865 slavery was sent back to hell in the United States from whence is sprang. I believe in the land of the free and home of he brave. But inasmuch we have but little law enforcement in the right direction in Scott County Mississippi, and most of the persecution law, pass and I hands-off this up to you. A nest of kinsfolk's here will soon let you know that hell is and ice-house when you seek to investigate slavery and moon shining and bootlegging. If we had one Federal officer in this part of Mississippi who himself was bootleggers and moonshiners about Sebastopol also. No State officer will do anything with them in Scott County. We think it is not right to advertise our part we play in the matter to the slave-holders, as we don't want to be forced make a slave of any one or more of them. The banker here is a kinsman to the nest. If the Negro boy is taken and carried off away from them he will Negro slave, serving his time in bonds to a dominating master.

Your truly,
Coherk L. McClendon

Any many other slaves over Mississippi, Alabama and Ga., being smuggled.

Myron S. McNeil

Attorney and Counselor at Law

Hazlehurst, Miss

June Twenty-Seventy, 1927

United States District Attorney's Office

Washington, D.C.

Gentlemen:

John and Willie Douglass formerly of Copiah County, Mississippi, moved to Thornton, Mississippi, - what is designated in this section as the delta, -on the plantation of one Mr. S. J. Brown.

When the high water struck the delta these people made every effort to return to their home county, but were prevented from doing by their landlord. Recently they slipped away from there and moved to Copiah County, leaving their children there, six in number, the youngest being only two years of age. They claim the letter they write through the United States mail are intercepted by Mr. Brown and they were unable to get in communication with their children. This is one instance is hundreds of instance where Negroes from the hill counties are being forced to remain in the delta against their wills.

These Negroes were all originally from the hill counties, and when the boil weevil struck the hill countries the delta farmers and planters came into the hills and solicited all the labor to go to the delta, and it was released without objection by the hill farmer. I may add too that when the boll weevil struck the hill counties of Mississippi it was form more disastrous, financially speaking. than the flood struck the delta. Now then. These same people want to return to the hills. The vast majority of the delta planter are not undertaking to force these people against their will to remain in the delta, but a few of them are taking advantage of the situation and feel that they are being supported by the government in holding these people in a state of peonage.

In you will send some representative from the government to my office I will have a number of these people present to that he can interview then and ascertain for himself the condition prevails. These Negroes are being maintained by the Red Cross when as matter of fact they would not ask for this assistance if they were released and given and opportunity to procure work in hills

#2-USDA

I am enclosing letter from the Red Cross to this effect

Yours very truly

M.R. McNeil

MYRON S. McNEIL
Attorney and Counselor at Law
HAZLEHURST, MISS.

June Twenty-Seventh,

1 9 2 7.

United States District Attorney's Office,
Washington,
D.C.

Gentlemen:

John and Willie Douglass, formerly of Copiah County,
Mississippi, moved to Thornton, Mississippi, - what is designated in
this section as the delta, - on the plantation of one, Mr.S.J.Brown.

When the high water struck the delta these people
made every effort to return to their home County, but were prevented
from doing so by their landlord. Recently they slipped away from
there and moved to Copiah County, leaving their children there, six
in number, the youngest being only two years of age. They claim
that letters they write through the United States mail are intercepted
by Mr. Brown and that they are unable to get in communication with
their children. This is one instance in hundreds of instances where
negroes from the hill counties are being forced to remain in the
delta against their wills.

These negroes were all originally from the hill counties, and when the boll weevil struck the hill counties the delta
farmers and planters came into the hills and solicited all this
labor to go to the delta, and it was released without objection by
the hill farmers. I may add too that when the boll weevil struck
the hill counties of Mississippi it was far more disastrous, financially
speaking, than when the flood struck the delta. Now then, these same
people want to return to the hills. The vast majority of the delta
planters are not undertaking to force these people against their
will to remain in the delta, but a few of them are taking advantage
of the situation and feel that they are being supported by the government in holding these people in a state of peonage.

If you will send some representative from the government to my office I will have a number of these people present so
that he can interview them and ascertain for himself the condition
that prevails. These negroes are being maintained by the Red Cross,
when as a matter of fact they would not ask for this assistance if
they were released and given an opportunity to procure work in the

12

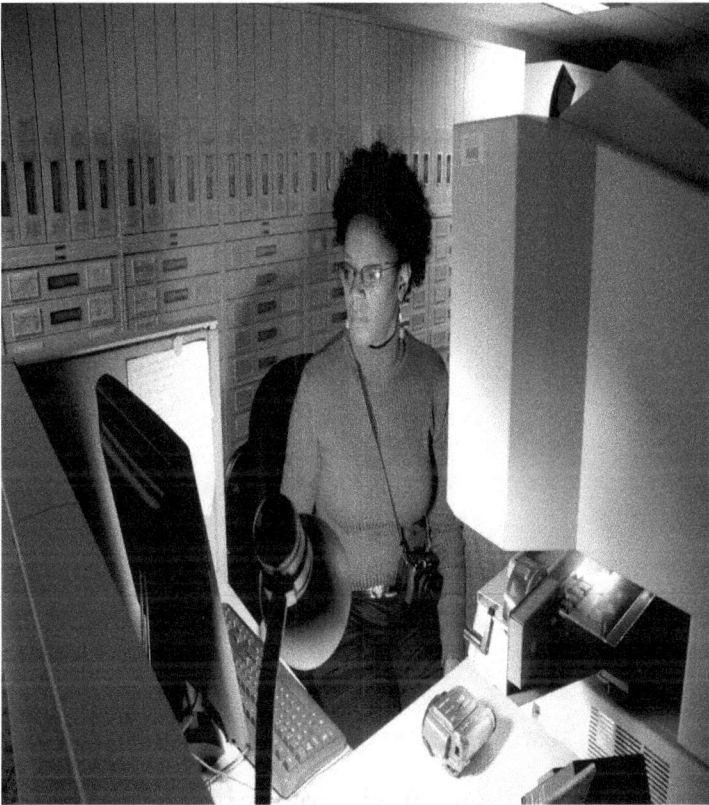

Antoinette Harrell at the National Archives conducting peonage
Involuntary Servitude and Slavery Research
Photo Credit: Walter C. Black, Sr.

Attorney-At-Law

East St. Louis, Illinois

June 11, 1928

U.S. Attorney General

Washington, D.C.

Dear Sir:

N.W. Parden

Rev. H.H. Harris, formerly of Hickman County, near the town of Tipton, Tennessee, was employed to work upon the farm of one Reuben Tipton, in Kentucky, Kentucky on shares. After working a few months, a disagreement arose between Harris and Mr. Tipton, and he felt that it was best to leave the farm. Mr. Tipton objected and defied him to leave, and at the time there was no indebtedness between the two men, and to escape, Mr. Harris had to leave during the night, stealing two of his small children, and leaving his wife and a six-year old son on the farm.

He and his family was forced to work on the farm of the said Tipton without pay; that the wife of the said Harris is not being held on the farm, and forced to work for the said Tipton without pay. That Harris was forced by circumstances, and threats to leave all of his personal property, which amount to seven or eight hundred dollars. Mr. Harris made complaint to U.S. District Attorney, located at Louisville, Kentucky to assist him, or to bring suit against Tipton, but some reason he has refused; he also made complaint before U.S. Commissioner at Paducah, Kentucky, and received no assistance there, and for that reason he is now appealing to you to see if it is in your power to order and direct the District Attorney to Louisville, Kentucky to take some action to release him of his present and unfortunate position.

Owning to the reputation of the said Tipton for holding men on his farm as peons, and ass to the many deaths of Negroes, who have attempted to leave his farm, he is in fear of trying, personally, to relieve himself, or to get his wife away, as the knows that it will cost him his life to make and attempt.

Mr. Harris is now located at Cairo, Ill., and here in my office seeking information as to what should be done. So, I am writing you to give him all the assistance possible. Mr. Harris, I understand, it a Minister of the Gospel; a man of culture and refinement, and is seeking immediate relief, if any you can give.

Very respectfully,

N.W. Parden

NWP: B

Cooley & Parsons
Attorney and Counsellor at Law

Jefferson, GA.

March 24th, 1908

United States Attorney General

Washington D.C.

Dear Sir:

In the interest of suffering humanity, I wish to call your attention to the fact that there is a Negro in this City by name of Claud Cooper who is being held involuntary servitude by one Branch, and is hiring the Negro out against (negro's will) and getting the proceeds of his labor.

The negro in question, came into my Offices yesterday to get Legal Advise as to leaving this man and was not in my Office but a few minutes until the man holding him came in and told the negro that he need not be trying to leave; that he was going to keep the negro regardless of what the negro did, hire him out and get the proceeds of the negro's labor. The man admitted that he has been working the Negro contrary to, and against the Negro's will.

This negro is 17 years, had no Guardian, or adopted by any one, and has been held by this man for a number of years against his will without every having been sent to School a day, and at present, is in rags and tatters barely sufficient to hide his nakedness-not having a change of clothing.

The way this Negro is being treated is ordeal enough to raise the indignation of any Christian community. He had to go thru that severe sleet during January and February without shoes, and was compelled to work bare feet and in clothing mention above.

Should you send a Secret Service Man to this place to investigate this case, please advise him to call me to his Hotel when the gets here.

Owing to the fact that most of Southern Officials are little slow to prosecute Peonage cases. I called this cases to your attention, and reported it to Henry E. Thomas, Secret Service Operative, Charlotte, N.C in order that you might get behind it and have it thoroughly investigated.

Should you want to know about veracity, before going into

and investigation of his case, conferred with J. M. Millikan, U.S. Marshall, Greensboro, N.C., under whom I served from March 1901 to April 1st, 1906.

Trusting that you will, in the interest of suffering humanity, take interest in the case and have same thoroughly investigated, I am,

Most truly yours,

Joseph A. Parson

Loyal A. Goins

Attorney-At-Law

Notary, Collections and Fire Insurance

Office to N. Ontario St.

Toledo, Ohio

April 11, 1921

Hon. Warren G. Harding

President of the United States

Washington, D.C.

Dear Sir:

I wish to thank you for the recent investigation and
discovery made in the case of John. S. Williams of Jasper
County Georgia for the murder of slaves, held on his
plantation and beg of you to continue to make like
investigation, throughout the entire South as I am informed
that many like cases exist.

Respectfully,

Loyal A. Goins

Department of Justice

Office of United States Attorney

Eastern District of Louisiana

Customhouse Building

New Orleans La, August 28, 1912

The Attorney General
Washington, D.C.

Sir:

Several weeks ago, complain was made to me by one Matt Briscoe, a Negro about the manner in which he had been treated and held in custody at Bogalusa. One cannot always rely on the accuracy of the statements of such complaints, but the facts as stated by Briscoe, seem to show outrageously unjust treatment, and there is a possibility of the facts as stated by him justifying a prosecution under Section 19 of the Criminal Code, for conspiracy to deprive one of his liberty, guaranteed under the Constitutions and laws of the United States The prosecution, however, would not have been justified without evidence to substantiate the facts stated by Briscoe.

I called in Special Agent Harris when Briscoe state then, and requested Mr. Harris to make the investigation. I am interested in the successful prosecution of such cases, and I know the Department is also, but it is useless to go into them without through preparation. Up to this time, Mr. Harris has not investigated the case, or at least, he has not made any report of same to me. I am not writing this in the nature of a complaint against Mr. Harris, because it may be that the Department has kept this busy on other matters, such as violations of the Neutrality laws, which he considers important, but which, to my mind, are not as important as such complaints as Briscoe's

Respectfully, United States Attorney

Department of Justice

Office of United States Attorney

Northern District of Mississippi

Oxford

November 6th, 1912

Sir:

On the 1st inst, this office received a letter from Special Agent S.N. Allred written from Greensboro, Alabama , enclosing copy of this report in re W.A. Thornton for alleged violation of the Peonage Laws, near Doddsville, County of Sunflower, State of Mississippi, Northern District thereof, and this office has today subpoenaed the witnesses named in said investigation report, to be and appear before the Grand Jury of the United States Court which meets at Oxford Mississippi the first Monday in December, at which time this matter shall have a thorough investigation before the Grand Jury.

Respectfully,

W. E. Stone

Asst. U.S. Attorney

Department of Justice

Office of the United States Attorney

Middle District of Alabama, Montgomery

New Brockton, Ala. R #1

May 31, 1910

Mr. Warren Reese,

Dear Sir:

I will say in reply to your letter in regard to B.J. Stevens holding negro in Peonage I do not know as I know what Peonage is, but to my knowledge Mr. Steven had a negro for something over 3 years that has run away several times & he would put out a reward for him & get him back & put him to work. Mr. Steven kept this Negro said Mr. Stevens never paid him anything for this work. I have heard it talked in this settlement that Mr. Stevens whipped this Negro.

Yours truly,

(Signed) L.J. Blair

Antoinette Harrell conducting peonage research
National Archives
College Park, Maryland
Photo Credit: Walter C. Black, Sr.

Department of Justice

Office of the United States] Attorney

Middle District of Alabama] Montgomery

New Brockton, R.F.D. #1

5/26/10

Hon. Warren S. Reese,

U.S. Attorney] Montgomery, Ala.

Dear Sir:

In reply to yours of 21st inst. Will say that I do not know what constitutes Peonage] but if forcing negroes to stay with, and forcing them to work with a person, in peonage], Mr. B.J. Stephens, has come to my places after his negro several times, drove him home and whipped him. I have seen the scars on the Negro where whipped him. I have the scars on the Negro where they whipped him. The Negroes are deathly afraid of Mr. Stephens. They say he will not pay them for their work. Every time the Negroes run away from Mr. Stephen, he puts up a reward, gets him back, beats] him and puts back to work. Considering then existing circumstance, it has been talked in the community for some time that it is a wonder that Mr. Stephens do not get into trouble about the way he manage negroes.

I have been living here something over three years. Mrs. Stephens had a Negro at that time with him by the name of Frank Danzie Frank ran off several times, and upon Mr. B. J. Stephens offering reward, the Negro was brought and whipped;

The darkey has come to me and tried to get me to help him get away, said if he run off Mr. Stephens would put out a reward, get him back and beat him, or kill him, so he was afraid to try. The Negro has tried to get other to help him get away. When Mr. Stephen would get Frank back he was not allowed to go about alone for weeks at a time.

Your truly,

(Signed) J. Duff Reeves

Department of Justice

Office of United States Attorney

Eastern District of Louisiana

Customhouse Building

New Orleans, LA February 8, 1913

The Attorney General,

Washington, D.C.

Sir:

Mr. Horace Wilkinson a reputable citizen of Port Allen, Louisiana, who is the owner of the Poplar Grove Plantation at or near that point, called at this office today and reported that he believes the Peonage

Laws are being violated by sawmill owners and timber operators at Grabow, Merryville and several other points in Southwest, Louisiana. He reports that the agents of theses operators have been systematically inducing laborers (principally negro laborers) to leave Baton Rouge and the plantation in its vicinity, under agreements or contracts of employment with the operators. He says that personal investigation made by him reveal the fact that cash money is advanced to these laborers, to induce them to leave Baton Rouge, and that the further inducement of high wages in held out to them, and that when the agents of the operators obtain a sufficient number of laborers is this way, they are placed in railroad cars chartered fro the purpose and taken from Baton Rouge to Merryville and other in Calcasieu parish, and there held in involuntary servitude. Mr. Wilkinson says that these operations have become quite.

Other reports have reached this office from labor leaders who were interested in the recent labor riots and troubles in Gabow Louisiana. These also indicated that the operations of these sawmill and timber men are quite extensive. These facts seem to indicate that the timber worker are using these means to systemically fill the vacancies made in their camps] by the recent strikes, and would also seem to indicate that their mistreatment of the laborers this obtained is responsible for the riots and other labor troubles in the that territory.

The writer called Mr. Billups Harris Special Agent of

the Bureau of Investigation of the Department into the conference with Mr. Wilkinson so that Mr. Harris might be familiar with all the details, because it is believed that it will be very necessary for Mr. Harris to visit Baton Rouge and the Merryville district, in order to make a thorough personal investigation of the condition there. Mr. Wilkinson had promised to aid Mr. Harris in every way possible to obtain the necessary evidence, and has suggested the names of several other persons who might be able to co-operate with him. Mr. Wilkinson promises to make some further investigations on his own account, and that he will be able to report his findings to this office within the next week or tens days.

I wish to report these facts to the Department of, in order that we may be prepared to have Special Agent Harris act as early as possible after we hear further form Mr. Wilkinson, and I request Department to authorize him to set aside some of the other matters upon which he may be engaged, so as to avoid any interference with his work on this important case. The writer wishes also to present the situation to the Department as it appears to him, so that the

Department many determine whether or not it will be necessary to have some other agent assigned to the duty of assisting Mr. Harris in his investigation, particularly since Mr. Wilkinson's statement lead the writer to believe that one agent might not be able to cope with the situation.

I am sending a copy of this letter to the United States Attorney for the Western District of Louisiana, because it seems to me that while the laborers are being moved out of Baton Rouge in the Eastern District, the evidence might show that the offenses are being committed entirely within the Western District, since it seems, from what Mr. Wilkinson says, that these trains, after leaving Baton Rouge, go direct to Merryville, Louisiana, within the Western District, and if there is any violation of the Peonage Laws, such violation occurs, necessarily, in that District,

Respectfully,

For the United States Attorney,

Assistant United States Attorney

Department of Justice

M.D.P., -W.S.G.

53149

March 24, 1905

D.G. Maxwell, Esq.,

United States Commissioner

Charlotte, N.C

Sir:

I am in receipt of your letter of the 21st instant, relative in a violation of a statue of the State of North Carolina on the part of the City Recorder of the City of Charlotte, in sentencing Negro women to the county chain-gang for trivial offenses. From the information contained in your letter, it does not appear to me that the alleged offense is violation of a Federal statue and one of which the Federal government can take cognizance. However, I have referred the matter to the United States Attorney for the Western District of North Carolina for his information.

Respectfully,

Attorney General

M.D.I.,-W.S.C.

33149

March 24, 1905.

D. G. Maxwell, Esq.,

United States Commissioner,

Charlotte, N. C.

Sir:

I am in receipt of your letter of the 21st instant, relative to a violation of a statute of the State of North Carolina on the part of the City Recorder of the City of Charlotte, in sentencing negro women to the county chain-gang for trivial offenses. From the information contained in your letter, it does not appear to me that the alleged offense is a violation of a Federal statute and one of which the Federal government can take cognizance. However, I have referred the matter to the United States Attorney for the Western District of North Carolina for his information.

Respectfully,

Attorney General.

Department of Justice.

.... N.C. .... Dated Mch. 21, 1905.

From D.C.Maxwell,
U.S.Comr.

SUBJECT:

Complains that City Recorder,
Charlotte, N.C., is sentencing
negro women to chain-gang.

Referred to   W.D.C.

ACTION:

Answer & to the U.S.
atty., Wn N.C.,
March 24, 1905.

March 24, 1905

D.G. Maxwell, Esq.,

United States Commissioner

Charlotte, N.C

Sir:

I am in receipt of your letter of the 21st instant, relative in a violation of a statue of the State of North Carolina on the part of the City Recorder of the City of Charlotte, in sentencing Negro women to the county chain gang for trivial offenses. From the information contained in your letter, it does not appear to me that the alleged offense is violation of a Federal statue and one of which the Federal government can take cognizance. However, I have referred the matter to the United States Attorney for the Western District of North Carolina for his information.

Respectfully,

Attorney General

I think, and have so recommended to our District Attorney that this man should be brought to trial.

I have been United States Commissioner since Mr. Cleveland's first term as President and have never know such a flagrant violation of the law. There will be no trouble in getting the necessary evidence.

Your truly.

GD.E. Maxwell

U.S. Commissioner.

Peonage Files at the National Archives

Jackson, Miss.

Department of Justice,

Washington, D. C.

The Department should make an investigation of some matters in Smith and Simpson counties in this state. On the line between Smith and Simpson near what is known as Sullivans Hollow lives a man by the name of Ware (W. T. I think) who has several sons and a son-in-law by the name of Turner. It is reported that the Wares have been stealing negro boys and selling them over in the Delta. One of the young Wares is a Dr. over there and was to dispose of them. The Wares were arrested and tried at Mize, Miss. for kidnapping a boy and hiding him out at the home of Turners over in Simpson until they could get him off to the Delta. Wares att'ys got him out of it without letting all the facts come out.

Turner over in Simpson has a brother-in-law whos father has had an old negro, Allen Ward, under bondage for several years. Allen left his master, W. C. Burns, last year and Burns and his boys one of them being the brother-in law of Turner, went down in Jefferson Davis County and found the old negro and brought him back to Burne's home near Magee under a gard with a gun. The came back the public road and a negro by the name of Durr who lives near King. Durr saw them with the gun. J. P. Purser, Parson Jones col, Ed. King col. Noah McWilliams and his sons all living near Magee can tell a lot about this.

Any one sent to investigate these matters should have due regard with whom this matter is discussed for in both cases there are a lot of kin folks about who would not give them away. The J. P. records at Magee and Mize both will show the names of some parties who can give some information if they will do so.

Boys stolen in Simpson and Smith Counties, Mississippi by the Wares and disposed of in the Mississippi Delta

CHAPTER TWO

LETTERS TO UNITED STATES PRESIDENTS

LETTER FROM GOVERNOR

President Calvin Coolidge
President Franklin D. Roosevelt
President Warren Harding
Governor Earl Brewer

Mississippi

Executive Department Jackson

April 8th, 1915

Dear Mr. Lee:

I am handling you a letter form a darkey, which is
rather difficult to read, but which refers, to the force
detention of a family on the plantation of Mr. Sell Jones, at
or near Sharkey, Miss. I will state that within the past
month at least five Negroes have been to me with pitiful
tales as to the way they have been beaten up and the
statement that they had to flee for their lives leaving their
families on this place. Once of them was caught after
gotten some miles away and carried back there forcibly. It
looks as if peonage was practiced on the is place to quite
and extent and if your department could make and

Investigation I believe you will unearth a bad condition there. I know it is a difficult matter to get evidence in such cases but that you will do all in your power I am confident.

Sincerely,
Earl Brewer
Governor

THE TALMAGE HOUSE

RATES $2.00 PER DAY

BATH ROOMS, ELECTRIC LIGHTS
AND INSIDE TOILETS. BETWEEN
MO. PACIFIC AND KATY DEPOTS.

PEON CASES TO ROOSEVELT.

The President's Aid Sought to Stop Florida Slavery.

WASHINGTON, Oct. 14.—Charges that peonage and slave holding of the most flagrant character exist in the southern part of Florida undetected by the federal officers of that state have been made by Miss Emma Sterling of Tampa, secretary of the Florida Humane association, who came to Washington to lay the results of her investigations before the President. She will see the President tomorrow and ask him to investigate the peonage charges.

It is said at the White house that the matter will be placed in the hands of the Department of Justice, which will institute an investigation through the district attorney's office for the Southern Florida district.

Miss Sterling is more than 70 years old and has been for the past ten years a citizen of Florida. She has advocated for years the repeal of certain laws on the state statute books with reference to the leasing of state convicts. She spoke freely to-day of the conditions she hoped to remedy.

"First of all," she said, "I want to get this matter in the hands of the President and enlist his help. The Humane association of Florida proposes to put a stop to this slave holding and it has sent me here to present to the powers that be every fact which will aid them in prosecuting the guilty persons.

"Those responsible for these helpless black and white slaves are not residents of Florida, but come from a far distant state. The convict labor in itself is really slave holding, for the treatment inflicted on the convicts by those who buy them for a term of months or years, as though they were merchandise cattle, is inhuman in the extreme.

"We are trying to stop that thing, but the state delights to traffic in this sort of business, and the association is powerless.

"But we are fighting now to free gangs of men who are held absolutely in a state of bondage, who were carried into the state like mules, and are kept under the lash at hard labor, and who are given barely enough to live on."

A FALL RESTORED HER SIGHT.

After One Accident Had Made a Woman Blind Another Made Her See.

LONDON, Oct. 14.—A strange case of sight which was destroyed by one accident being restored by another is reported from Leeds. One day twenty-two years ago,

Franklin D. Roosevelt
32nd President of the United States

29th Warren G. Harding
29th President of the United States

Calvin Coolidge
30th President of the United States

MISSISSIPPI

EXECUTIVE DEPARTMENT
JACKSON

EARL BREWER
GOVERNOR

W. J. BUCK

April 8th., 1915

Hon. C. R. Lee,

U. S. District Attorney,

Jackson, Miss.

Dear Mr. Lee:--

        I am handing you a letter from a darkey, which is rather difficult to read, but which refers to the forced detention of a family on the plantation of Mr. Sell Jones, at or near Sharkey, Miss. I will state that within the past month at least five negroes have been to me with pitiful tales as to the way they have been beaten up and the statement that they had to flee for their lives leaving their families on this place One of them was caught after having gotten some miles away and carried back there forcibly. It looks as if peonage was practiced on this place to quite an extent and if your department could make an investigation I believe you would unearth a bad condition there. I know it is a difficult matter to get evidence in such cases but that you will do all in your power I am confident.

                Sincerely

                Governor

175660

46

Catholic Laymen Association

June 13, 1921

Hon. Warren G. Harding

President of the United States

Washington, D.C.

Dear Mr. President

You will be interested in the enclosed copy of the Columbia Sentinel, published at Thomson, Ga. The Junior Senator form Georgia is the editor of this paper.

Your particular attention is directed to the matter under the head: Some very Interesting Editorial Notes on State and National Affairs, " which roads is follow:

The National Congress of Mothers, assembled at Washington, April 27th, filed a plea for 'missing girl."

We learn that sixty five thousand girls disappeared from their homes last year, and nothing is known of their whereabouts.

A great majority of these girls where captured by Catholic Priests and sentenced to slavery in the House of the Good Shepherd, etc.

In Keiley's establishment at Savannah, Ga., there may probably be score or more of those 'missing girls.'

The laws of Georgia require that Bishop Keiley's slave pen shall be inspected by officers of the courts of Chatham County , but the Bishop of Savannah informs us that he gets his laws from Rome, and therefore, he cannot recognize laws made in this country.

The question is, Shall Bishop Keiley be permitted to continue to laugh at our laws? Catholic Priests have no right to lure innocent girls into captivity, where they become victims of Priestly immorality.

The Bishop of Savannah has no right to run a "peonage farm" with his jurisdiction. Sixty-five thousand girls are lost in our big cities each year; they fall into traps set for them by Rome. Our laws owe them protection. Priests who are not permitted to marry, should not be allowed to capture young maidens and use them to satisfy lustful desires.

You will observe that the leading article on this page states that 'it remains to be seen whether the people of this country shall be blinded by the hypocrisies and false pretenses of Warren G. Harding as they were by those of Woodrow Wilson " and that the Roman Catholic Church dictates to Harding, just as it dictated to Wilson."

CATHOLIC LAYMEN'S ASSOCIATION OF GEORGIA

PUBLICITY DEPARTMENT
107 NINTH ST.
AUGUSTA, GEORGIA

JUN 15 1921

June 13, 1921.

Hon. Warren G. Harding,
President of the United States,
Washington, D.C.

Dear Mr. President:

You will be interested in the enclosed copy of the Columbia Sentinel, published at Thomson, Ga. The Junior Senator from Georgia is the editor of this paper.

Your particular attention is directed to the matter under the head: "Some Very Interesting Editorial Notes on State and National Affairs," which reads as follows:

The National Congress of Mothers, assembled at Washington, April 27th, filed a plea for "missing girls."

We learn that sixty five thousand girls disappeared from their homes last year, and nothing is known of their whereabouts.

A great majority of these girls were captured by Catholic Priests and sentenced to slavery in the Houses of the Good Shepherd, etc.

In Keiley's establishment, at Savannah, Ga., there may probably be a score or more of those "missing girls."

The laws of Georgia require that Bishop Keiley's slave pen shall be inspected by officers of the courts of Chatham County, but the Bishop of Savannah informs us that he gets his law from Rome, and, therefore, he cannot recognize laws made in this country.

The question is, Shall Bishop Keiley be permitted to continue to laugh at our laws?

Catholic Priests have no right to lure innocent girls into captivity, where they become victims of Priestly immorality.

The Bishop of Savannah has no right to run a "peonage farm" within his jurisdiction.

Sixty-five thousand girls are lost in our big cities each year; they fall into traps set for them by Rome.

Our laws owe them protection. Priests who are not permitted to marry, should not be allowed to capture young maidens and use them to satisfy lustful desires.

You will observe that the leading article on this page states that "it remains to be seen whether the people of this country shall be blinded by the hypocricies and false pretenses of Warren G. Harding, as they were by those of Woodrow Wilson," and that "the Roman Catholic Church dictates to Harding, just as it dictated to Wilson."

50

William Henry Huff

Director

Abolish Peonage Committee of America

Chicago, Illinois

Nov 25, 1994

Hon. Franklin D. Roosevelt

President

The White House

Washington, D.C.

Dear Mr. President

The enclosed from Lonnie Kimbrough a Negro with reference to this being held to a condition of peonage by one Mr. W. P. Scruggs in Sunflower County, Mississippi, is self-explanatory. I have talked with Mr. Kimbrough at length, and I am convinced that he was held to a

Condition of peonage as alleged.

Mr. President I think you know by now that the Negro people of this country are looking to you for a new emancipation so that new form of slavery know as peonage which entered the back door as the Proclamation of immirtal Lincoln drove chattel slavery out of the front door, should be abolished now for all time to come and we believe you will do it as no other can.

There are laws on the statue books sufficient to wipe it away. These laws only need to be vigorously enforced. I believe you will do it, and I am trusting that you will cause a sweeping investigation of the charges alleged in this affidavit, and if the facts warrant, prosecute to the limit.

Thanking you and wishing for another four years of success as our Chief Executive and Commander and Chief of the Army and Navy, I beg to remain.

William Henry Huff

520 E. 35th Street

PEON CASES TO ROOSEVELT

The President's Aid Sought to Stop Florida Slavery

Washington, Oct 14-Charges that peonage and slave holding of the most flagrant characters exist in the southern part of Florida undetected by the federal officers of the state have been made by Miss Emma Sterling of Tampa secretary of the Florida Humane Association, who came to Washington to lay the results of her investigations before the President She will see President tomorrow and ask him to investigate the peonage charges.

It is said at the White House that the matters will be placed in the hand of the Department of Justice which will institute an investigation through district attorney's office for the Southern Florida district.

Miss Sterling is more than 70 years old and has been for the past ten years a citizen of Florida. She has advocated for years the repeal of certain laws on the state statue books with reference to the leasing of state convicts. She spoke freely to-day of the conditions she hoped to remedy. "First of all," she said, " I want to get this matter in the hands of the President and enlist his help. The Humane association of Florida proposes to put a stop to this slave holding and it has sent me here to present to the powers that be every fact, which will aid them in prosecuting the guilty persons.

"Those responsible for these helpless black and white slaves are not residents of Florida but come from a far distant state. The convict labor in itself is really slave holding for the treatment melted out to the convicts by those who buy them for a term of months of years, as though they where purchasing cattle, inhuman in the extreme.

We are trying to stop that thing, but the state delights to traffic in this sort of business, and the association in powerless.

"But we are fighting now to free gangs of men who are held absolutely in a state of bondage., who were carried into the state like mules, and are kept under the lash at hard labor, and who are give barely enough to live on."

NATIONAL ASSOCIATION FOR THE ADVANCEMENT
OF COLORED PEOPLE

April 11, 1921

Hon. Warren G. Harding

President of the United States

Washington, D.C.

Mr. dear Mr. President

I am sending you enclosed and editorial from the New
York Times of this morning on the peonage cases in Jasper,
County, Ga., and peonage in general as it relates to the
Department of Justice.

I am very anxious that this editorial should meet your
personal attention.

Very truly yours.

NATIONAL ASSOCIATION FOR THE

ADVANCEMENT OF COLORED PEOPLE

70 FIFTH AVENUE, NEW YORK

March 29, 1921

Hon. Warren G. Harding

President of the United States

Washington, D.C.

Dear Sir:

Yesterday we sent you the following telegram:

"The National Association for the Advancement of Colored People urgently requests of you that through investigation be made by the Department by Federal laws of peonage conditions in the Jasper County, Georgia where John Williams regarding peonage. This case is not an isolated one, but is indicative of similar conditions, which exist in most Southern states and particularly in the Mississippi Delta Henry Lowry, colored, was burned at the stake in most horrible fashion in Arkansas on held in peonage. In Philips County, Arkansas, in October 1919, an unknown number of Negroes were slaughtered and others of the State. This Association has furnished numerous cases of peonage to the Department of Justice. The entire economic future of the South and of America are affected by this system.

Through investigation and punish of those guilty of perpetuating this system whatever the cost to the United States, must be made. We urge you to issue such an order.

Sincerely yours,

James Weldon Johnson

Secretary

S.D. Redmond

Attorney at Law

217-218 Redmond Building

Jackson, Miss.

April 30, 1927

President Calvin Coolidge

Washington, D.C.

Dear Mr. President

This is to call your attention to the alleged peonage

now existing in the Flood "Relief" camps at Vicksburg,
Yazoo City, and other points in Mississippi where flood
refugees are held.

These people are hurdled in camps of 5000 or more and
soldiers from the National Guard are used to let none out of

those camps and to keep people on the outside form coming
in and talking with them. And it is said that the condition of
non-communication is to continue until the water subside
and these "free" people can be hurdled back to the plantation.

Well, of course, such a state of affair needs no argument to a man like you.

It said that many relief boats have hauled whites only have gone to imperiled districts and taken all whites, out and left the Negroes; it

is also said that the planters in some instances point of a gun for fear they would get away and not return.

In other instances, it is said mules have been given preference on boats to Negroes left in peril.

It is said that the people in these camps are sorely in need of more of the necessaries of life; namely, blankets, clothing proper food. While the Red Cross is doing much it is by no mean without criticism. One of it's great mistakes it that it tries to run things without spending money. Well, of course, that is a most grievous error when human life and health are in stake.

Under such circumstances the value of honey must necessarily pale into insignificance, and yet they attempt to get all their work done without paying anything for it. As you will agree, that only adds delay and increased suffering.

This is given in the strictest confidence, but with the hope that you will please have what I have said look into.

The enclosed clipping is self-explanatory. With very best wishes and kindest regards, I am.

Very truly yours.

S. D. Redmond

CHAPTER THREE

ELEVEN NEGROES MURDERED ON WILLLIAMS PLANTATION

New York City.

April 1, 1921

Mr. James Weldon Johnson, Secretary

National Assn. for the Advancement of Colored People

70 Fifth Avenue,

Sir:

The Department is in receipt of your telegram of March 28 and your letter of March 29, in regard to the case of John Williams, of Jasper County, Georgia, charged with killing of several Negroes. It may interest you to know that the facts in connection therewith were discovered by agents of this Department.

The Department is also engaged in the investigation of a number of other cases involving alleged violation of the Peonage Law.

Respectfully,

R.P. Stewart

Assistant Attorney General

Department of Justice

Office of United Stated Attorney

April 18, 1921

The Attorney General

Washington, D.C.

Sir:

I reply to your letter of April 11th, (RPS RCMcH 50-442-20) in which you desire me to have and investigation made as to whether any of the officials of the City Prison or local courts of Atlanta, where is collusion with the William family in the removal of negroes from the City Prison of Atlanta to the Williams' farm in Jasper County.

Foremost to your instructions, I called the attention of the Bureau of Investigation to this matter, and I am to-day in receipt of information from the Agent in Charge, in which he advised me that the feature of the investigations will be clearly brought out when the report is submitted to me as to the investigation, and that such comprehensive report of the entire matter will be transmitted to this office at an early date.

The Special Agent in Charge states further in his communication that he suppose me to be fully aware of the fact that the practice of paying negroes out of imprisonment is a very general one, and the he doubts seriously whether the prison officials can be charged with complicity, or even with knowledge of the fact that the released negroes in such case are to be held in peonage.

It is true, as stated by the Agent of the Bureau, that the practice of taking Negroes out of penal establishment is common. The practice takes various of forms, and I have never known before or any case of exactly this sort, where municipal prisoners are taken out and carried away from the municipality.

Very grave abuse in this line are other practiced and this office has been concerned on the subject. As soon as I get full information about the facts in this particular case, I will present indictments if the facts warrant. I have heretofore, however, called your attention to the fact that indict the Williams in this District is not strictly necessary. I have in various cases, proposed indictment, where peons are taken from the District into the Southern District, but that was because, in those cases. I apprehended that indictments would not be returned to the Southern District. Where the peonage takes places in one District, the normal venue would be in the District where the peonage occurred. In particular instances, however, it is sometimes necessary to indict in another District for illegal reasons.

The facts is in this particular cases have been partly laid before the Grand Jury in anticipation of the receipt of a full report on the subject. It is expected to present the balance of the fact as soon as the full report is received.

Respectfully

Hoaner Alexander, United States Attorney

Loyal A. Goins

Attorney-At-Law

Notary, Collections and Fire Insurance

Toledo, Ohio

April 11, 1921

Harry Daugherty

Atty, Gen. U.S.,

Washington, D.C.
Dear Sir:

    I wish to thank you for the recent investigation----very

Made in the case of John S. Williams of Jasper County Georgia for the murder of "Slaves" held on this plantation and beg of you to continue to make like investigations, throughout the entire Southland as I am informed that many others like cases exist.

        Respectfully
        Loyal A. Goins

LOYAL A. GOINS
ATTORNEY-AT-LAW
NOTARY, COLLECTIONS AND
FIRE INSURANCE

BELL PHONE, MAIN 8738   HOME PHONE, MAIN 3844 R
OFFICE 10 N. ONTARIO ST.

TOLEDO, OHIO.

50 442

April 11, 1921.

50-442-32

Hon. Harry Daugherty,
Atty. Gen. U. S.,
Washington, D. C.

Dear Sir:

I wish to thank you for the recent investigation made made in the case of John S. Williams, of Jasper county Georgia, for the murder of "slaves" held on his plantation, and beg of you to continue to make like investigations, throughout the entire Southland as I am informed that many other like cases exist. Respectfully,

Loyal A. Goins

CHAPTER FOUR

STATE OF GEORGIA
COUNTY OF FULTON

Personally appeared Jacob Osmanskey, on oath says: I am eighteen (18) years of age. I left New York five ago in company with about sixty mane, fifteen of who were Russian Jews, like myself, Miller & Company, a labor agency, 201 East Second Street, New York City, advertised that they would get jobs for us at $1.50 a day and board at a saw-mill in Alabama and that the saw-mill company would pay our railroad fare to the places. An agent of he saw-mill company, who is Smith & Company, Lockhart, Alabama, brought us by steamer from New York to Savannah, where another agent of the Company, a negro, met us and took us by train to Milner, Alabama, From there this negro, was a foreman for Smith & Company, took us by wagon to Lockhart, about twenty miles from Milner. We arrived there on a Saturday afternoon and were put in tents, eight men to the tent, tents being about 8' x 12'. On the following Monday morning we marched to the saw-mill, adjacent to the tents, in squads of five and was a Negro guard over each squad with a pistol and a strap. We were put to cutting trees. When we were not able to do the work the Negro would whip us. He whipped me several times on my head, eyes and back until I bled. He took off my trouser and whipped me in this manner. I was there five weeks and we would go from the tents to the saw-mill and from the saw-mill to the tents, and no more, every day. All of us ate together and we went to bed at night there were four guards who kept guard over us.

There was one fellow by the name of John Durbin who was still there. He tried to get away and they caught him and put him in a dark cellar and locked him there and fed him for three days on bread and water. Several other of the men were whipped for trying to get away.

STATE OF GEORGIA

COUNTY OF

George Fleming, being duly sworn, deposes and says: I am an American, unmarried and formerly lived in New York City, 348 W. 16th Street where my family now lives. I was working for " Crown Cordial Extract Company," 18 Desbrosses Street, New York City. I left because I couldn't stand the heat of the boilers—I came June 25to the South having been sent through Schwartz's agency.

When we were brought to the camp we found the work hard, and the living disgusting. They put me at kitchen work. While I was working for them several men escaped and the foremen captured them. I saw a hand car come back with the foreman and the prisoners were scared and afraid to speak. They had no dinner that day. I was engaged for railroad work and was put on "flunkie work" which is being to waiters, and then put as kitchen boy, then as serving the foreman's table, then helping the cook. I wanted to leave.

I did pick the shovel work form June 26th the July 7th till the second lot came down, then they changed me to the kitchen. The food was awful.

The bread was all blue moulded—we would have to out the bread crusts off to take the mould off and then when it was cut off we would taste the sour mould. This was all the bread they gave the boys.

At two in the morning I would have to get up to help cook and I stopped work at ten o'clock. The earliest I ever went to bed was eight o'clock. The meat was tripe, salted ham, and frankfurter. The boys threw the bad tripe.

STATE OF GEORGIA

COUNTY OF FULTON

Adolph Lapping, being duly sworn, disposes and says: I am a Russian, having come to this country about four months ago. On the 29th day of July, 1906, I lived at 65 East 98th Street, New York City, and having noticed an advertisement in the German, newspaper that from fifty to one hundred men were wanted for railroad work, I applied at the office of S.S. Schwartz in East First Street and was sent by him to Schwartz's office at 250 Bowery, Schwartz sent one of his men, a medium blonde man with light mustache, from First Street to the Bowery with me and in the Bowery office the business

arrangement were made. I did not sigh and paper and no contract was given me there. In one hour, same day, I went to the ship designated, and on the ship was give the annexed contract which was written by Schwartz on the ship.

About forty-five other men went on the same shame ship with me and when we arrived on Brunswick, Georgia, we were met by the four men form the Atlantic and Birmingham

Construction Company. We were then taken to a restaurant and day and night on train, which stopped in the woods near Offerman, forty miles from

Brunswick. Schwartz had said it was nice place for a jewelry maker.

STATE OF ILLINOIS

COUNTY OF COOK

Lonnie Kimbrough after being duly sworn, deposed and say that he is a citizen of the United States and that, to wit: on or about the 30th day of November, 1942 he, along with a number of other persons, including one Willie Stewart, was in the home of one Gus, whose surnames was then and is now unknown t o Affiant, where one those present remarked that "her is the town Negro working for the Government and making big money, while we poor devils are farm hands are just hands on Mr. Sam Harvey's plantation. Let's beat him up and take his money," at a which time Willie Stewart and his sons, "Frog," Johnnie B., and another whose name is not now know to Affiant, made a break toward Affiant, while Affiant backed out of the door and attempted to make a peaceful getaway.

Affiant further that these person all had knives except "Frog," and he had a short bench, with which he was striking at Affiant. I in the melee, Affiant was unable to get anything with which to protect himself except a bottle which he picked up, after he had been caught, and with which he attempted to ward off het blows and attempts at stabling.

Affiant further avers that his overcoat, already sent for as and exhibit, was cut in many places by the aforesaid hoodlums, and that one Mr. Robert Crook, ad white gentleman, forced these hoodlums to cease beating fingers, and the men were so busy cutting at Affiant, who was warding them off as best he could with his elbow, and the bottle aforesaid, that one of their own number, to wit: Willie Stewart, was said to have lost his eye in some way unknown to Affiant.

Affiant further avers that he was taken to jail and that Mr. Crook forced the police to take two of his tormentors to jail also; and that the aforesaid outlaw, otherwise known as "Frog," had not long before been released from the County Farm, where his boos, Mr. Harvey, has suffered him to go in order to teach him a lesson about being forever into malicious mischief or crime.

Affiant further avers that after spending one week in jail one Mr. W.P. Scruggs signed his bond, which was fixed at

$150.00, with the understanding that Affiant should go to Mr. Scruggs' plantation with his wife and children and remain there forever thereafter, whereupon Mr. Scruggs sent a truck to Affiants' house in Moorehead and move everything Affiant and his wife owned the plantation. This was in December 1942. Affiant then proceeded to make a crop, pretended upon the sharecropper plan, but after making 9 bales of cotton, 75 bushels of corn, 10 bushel of potatoes and all the other things commonly made on farms, Mr. Scruggs, at settlement time at the end of 1943, handed affiant only $42.00 as his share of the bumper crop. Affiant proceeded to make another crop in 1944 and did make such crop, but on or about the 28th of August, 1944, Affiant under-

----

---, made his escape to Chicago because he had been convinced, after nearly two years, the he was in a condition of peonage, involuntary servitude, slavery. Affiant knows of his knowledge that one Otis a Negro, asked Mr. Scruggs the privilege of moving and was beaten by Mr. Scruggs to insensibility with an axe handle, so much so that his arm was broken, whereupon Mr. Scrugg's sent him to a hospital for treatment and cure. This occurred in 1943. Affiant knows of his own knowledge that one Martin, whose given name he is unable to recall, went to Mr. Scruggs and asked that privilege of moving, and was beaten down with a lug wrench. This, Affiant heard with his own ears and saw with his own eyes. This occurred in 1944. Affiant know of his own knowledge at Mr. Scruggs made a break at Kino Johnson, a young Negro about 20 years of age, in order to beat him up for asking the privilege of moving from the plantation, and that Kino Johnson, being young and agile, outran Mr. Srcuggs and thereby saved himself from being beaten down. However, Mr. Scruggs ran in his house and secured something, either a pistol, or some other deadly instrument, the exact nature of which Affiant is unable to say because he was at some distance away, and ran toward Kino Johnson's house in search of Kino, but in vain.

Affiant further avers that there are a great number of Negroes on Mr. Scruggs' plantation in virtual slavery, many of whom are afraid to speak above a whisper lest they be beaten down or shot down.

Affiant further avers that it is common knowledge upon the plantation that Mr. Scruggs will beat Negroes to insensibility, shoot them, or do anything else he desires do to them without being molested by the law in any way and that it is common knowledge also that he shot one Negro eye out, and that he has been beating, shooting and otherwise maiming Negroes for a great number of years.

Affiant further avers that was guaranteed, not only by Mr. Scruggs, but by the lawyer whom his parents retained to represent him at the court-house in March, 1943, that there was absolutely nothing else to the case against him, and that all he had to do was to remain forever with his wife and children on Mr. Scruggs' plantation and make Mr. Scruggs a good hand; that he would never again, at anytime, be called in question about the affray which occurred between Affiant, Willie Stewart, and the Stewart sons in Moorehead, Mississippi on or about the 30th day of November, 1942.

Affiant further avers that all the above and foregoing took place in Sunflower County, Mississippi. Further Affiant sayeth not.

CHAPTER FIVE
NAACP PEONAGE FILES

National Association for the Advancement of Colored People

69 Fifth Avenue, New York

February 9, 1927

Hon. John G. Sargent, Attorney General

Department of Justice

Washington, D.C.

Dear Sir:

We are in receipt of a letter charging peonage practices
in Attala County, Mississippi. The letter names the Justice of
the Peace of Kosciusko and the constable, Jeff Thurrell, as
being in a "conspiracy" to arrest colored as well as white
people on trumped-up charges, fines imposed, it is alleged,
being paid by a saw mill and logging camp at Zama, also in
Attala County, which holds the prisoners indefinitely. The
letter further charges that Stephenson, Mississippi, is said to
be the worst quasi convict camp in the South. It is charged in
our correspondent's letter that the book of the Justice of the
Peace at Kosciusko, Miss., "show that every Negro who has
been before him has been given heavy fines." Peonage is

furthermore alleged to exist on the plantation of J.W. Cutrer and Sheriff Glass of Clarksdale, Mississippi; also in plantation in Coahoma County. I am enclosing the letter containing these charges, for your information and such action as you feel the matter warrants.

Very truly yours,

James Weldon
Secretary

NATIONAL ASSOCIATION FOR THE
ADVANCEMENT OF COLORED PEOPLE

69 FIFTH AVENUE, NEW YORK
(AT FOURTEENTH STREET)

TELEPHONE STUYVESANT 6548

JAMES WELDON JOHNSON,
SECRETARY
WALTER WHITE,
ASSISTANT SECRETARY

February 9, 1927

Hon. John G. Sargent, Attorney General
Department of Justice,
Washington, D. C.

Dear Sir:

The enclosed letter regarding peonage
in Mississippi was inadvertently left out of our
letter to you of this date.

Yours very truly,

Secretary

R

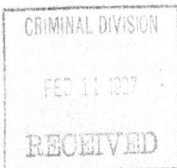

CRIMINAL DIVISION

FEB 11 1927

RECEIVED

50-48-3-2

CHAPTER SIX
BABIES FOR SALE

Department of Justice

United States Attorney

Oklahoma City

August 27, 1940

The Attorney General,

Washington, D.C.

 Attention, Hon. O. Johnson, Assistant Attorney General

Sir:

We desire to call your attention to what may be a violation of the provisions of the peonage statues or the provisions of the statues against involuntary servitude. We call your attention to the provisions of Section 446, Title 18 U.S.C.A., the second clause of which provides;

 * * * or whoever shall knowingly and willfully sell or cause to be sold, into any condition of involuntary servitude, any other person for any term whatever, *** shall be fined not more than $5000 and imprisoned not more than five years.

This is the section of the statue we have in mind. The

facts briefly are theses: A doctor by the name of J.G. Bailey who resides at 1604 Northwest 40th Street in Oklahoma City is engaged in operating a maternity home or hospital for unfortunate girls. We are advised that when the girls make their appearance at his establishment for the delivery of their prospective offspring's and for hospitalization, either then, or after the birth of the child, he required them execute in blank a consent for adoption.

We are further advised that he requires the girls to pay her hoard, keep, hospitalization and medical expenses if she is able to do so. After the child is born and the mother has left the hospital, the doctor is in custody of the offspring, and we are advised that he takes these children and finds prospective parents to whom he sells the child upon condition that will adopt the baby. We are advised that in one instance he sold a baby, which he did deliver for $35 on agreement that they would pay him and additional $40 as soon as the folks received the child. The people have never yet received their baby, and they are the ones who made the complaint.

The Attorney General #2

We further advised that in another instance he did deliver the baby and sold the child for a consideration of $300. When adoption proceeding were had, we are told that the doctor told the people to whom the child was sold to be sure and not tell Judge Blinn, the County Judge, about their purchase, for he wouldn't like it.

It occurs to the writer that the above quoted section of the Code could hardly apply to this situation. It seems that "servitude" would mean just that, and the care, education, custody and control of the infant would hardly be considered as being servitude. However, the County Attorney of this country has referred the matter to us, stating that the Oklahoma statues make no provision for cases of this nature, and unless there is some federal jurisdiction, he knows of no way in which this practice can be stopped.

Will you be kind enough to advise us as to your views in this matter, if there are any applicable provisions of the Code which we have overlooked, or any authorities which are in point, we should be glad to have them.

Thanking you, I am.

Very truly yours

Charles E. Dierker,

United States Attorney

ADDRESS REPLY TO
"UNITED STATES ATTORNEY"
AND REFER TO
INITIALS AND NUMBER

UNITED STATES ATTORNEY
WESTERN DISTRICT OF OKLAHOMA

OKLAHOMA CITY

August 27, 1940.

The Attorney General,
Washington, D. C.

Attention, Hon. O. John Rogge,
Assistant Attorney General

Sir:

We desire to call your attention to what may be a
violation of the provisions of the peonage statutes or the
provisions of the statutes against involuntary servitude.
We call your attention to the provisions of Section 446,
Title 18 U.S.C.A., the second clause of which provides:

"* * * or whoever shall knowingly and wilfully
sell or cause to be sold, into any condition
of involuntary servitude, any other person for
any term whatever; * * * shall be fined not more
than $5000 and imprisoned not more than five
years."

This is the section of the statute we have in mind.
The facts briefly are these: A doctor by the name of J. O. Bailey ,
who resides at 1604 Northwest 40th Street in Oklahoma City, is
engaged in operating a maternity home or hospital for unfortunate girls. We are advised that when the girls make their
appearance at his establishment for the delivery of their prospective offspring and for hospitalization, either at that time ,
or after the birth of the child, he requires them to execute in
blank a consent for adoption. We are further advised that he
also requires the girl to pay her board, keep, hospitalization
and medical expenses if she is able to do so. After the child
is born and the mother has left the hospital, the doctor is in
custody of the offspring, and we are advised that he takes these
children and finds prospective parents to whom he sells the
child upon condition that they will adopt the baby. We are advised that in one instance he sold a baby which he did not
deliver for $35 on agreement that they would pay him an addi-
tional $40 as soon as the folks received the child. These
people have never yet received their baby, and they are the
ones who made the complaint.

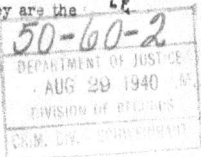

CHAPTER SEVEN
RAILROAD COMPANIES

Birmingham & Northwestern Railway Co.

Office of R.W. Hall, President

Memphis, Tenn., April 1, 1912

Mr. Casey Todd,

United States District Attorney,

Memphis, Tenn.,

My dear Sir:

Mr. J. W, Wright Jr., who home place seems to be Union Springs, Ala., had the contract for building the Birmingham & Northwestern Railroad from Jackson to Dyersburg, Tenn., and began the same on April 15th, last. It was the current report last summer along the line of road being built that negroes were made to work against their will, that they were held against their will, and that since they run away they were hunted like beasts, and if found were whipped and made to return to the Railroad camp. Mr. M.W. Ewell of this city, who was last year mayor of Dyersburg has some information concerning this, and so have many other parties along the line of road from here to Dyersburg. There is at work on the road now for the road, a Negro who was brutally whipped and who hid himself away in a boxcar, and has been afraid to go anywhere near the contractor's camp since that time. Negroes are usually very reticent about giving information that would be injurious to white people, and it seems that the government is the only authority, which commands their confidence sufficiently to get them to tell of their wrongs.

I am enclosing a letter just received from citizens of Memphis, I believe this letter to be absolutely true, from my knowledge of conditions that have existed in this contractor's camp. Since last spring he was kept with him I believe and carried from state to state Negroes who would gladly have left him at any time, but who have been held by fear to his bidding. I will give you every assistance in my power, if you think conduct of this contactor on this line of road. I would be glad after examining into the facts contained in the letter I enclose, that you would return it to me.

Yours very truly

R.M. Hall

3/1912   Copy

Mr. R.W. Hall

This may not concern you, though I was told and know of your connection with this work. About June, 1911, I had a son employed by J.W. Wright constructing the B. & N. R. R. of which you are the principal owner. This boy happened to an accident; at the time, he wanted to stop and see a doctor He says he was forced to work on until he was to blind he could not see any further, then he was sent away. He also says he was afraid to stop form what he had seem of others, he would have had bad luck. From the accident, he has completely lost the sight of his eyes, and he has cost me considerable money, and is still on my

hands the rest of his life.

If I don't hear from you. I will proceed legally.

A.J. Wilson
1269 McLemore Ave.,

(COPY)

BIRMINGHAM & NORTHWESTERN RAILWAY CO.

Office of R.M.Hall, President.

Jackson, Tenn., April 1, 1912.

Mr. Casey Todd,

    United States District Attorney,

      Memphis, Tenn.

My dear Sir:

    Mr. J. W. Wright, Jr., whose home place seems to be Union Springs, Ala., had the contract for building the Birmingham & Northwestern Railroad from Jackson to Dyersburg, Tenn., and began the same on April 15th, last. It was the current report last summer along the line of road being built that negroes were made to work against their will, that they were held against their will, and that since they ran away they were hunted like beasts, and if found were whipped and made to return to the Railroad camp. Mr. M. W. Ewell of this city, who was last year mayor of Dyersburg has some information concerning this, and so have many other parties along the line of road from here to Dyersburg.

    There is at work on this road now for the road, a negro who was brutally whipped and who hid himself away in a box car, and has been afraid to go any where near the contractor's camp since that time. Negroes are usually very reticent about giving information that would be injurious to white people, and it seems that the government is the only authority which commands their confidence sufficiently to get them to tell of their wrongs.

    I am enclosing a letter just received from a citizen of Memphis, I believe this letter to be absolutely true, from my knowledge of conditions that have existed in this contractor's camp. Since last spring he has kept with him I believe and carried from state to state negroes who would gladly have left him at any time, but who have been held by fear to his bidding. I will give you every assistance in my power, if you think it necessary, to have the United States Marshal investigate the conduct of this contractor on this line of road. I would be glad after examining into the facts contained in the letter I enclose, that you would return it to me.

                    Yours very truly,

              R. M. Hall.

Mountain Said to Be Shot
Down When They Try to Escape

Indictment Are Found
Federal Officers Seek the Contractors
and Their Aides: Witnesses Are Guarded by Armed Men

(By a Special Correspondent)

KNOXVILLE, TENN., Sept, 21-Their escape cut off by armed guards who shoot to kill, white men and women and negroes are being held as slaves in railroad camps in the mountains of eastern Tennessee.

They are compelled to work whether they are well or sick, and are beaten almost to death when they refuses, When they ask for pay they are told they " owe" the commissary department more than is coming to them. This is the evidence upon which United States secret service officials are working here.

Robert B. Oliver, a railroad contractor, brother of the W.J. Oliver, most prominent contractor in the south, who offered to dig the Panama canal. James and Marin Condon, superintendents employed by the Oliver: G.S. Nightbort, foreman: Gordon Harrison foreman and James Holland, "walking boss." Are being sought by deputy United States marshals armed with indictments charging them with peonage. All were connected with the camp operated by Oliver, known as Camp No. 5. This is one of the camps where, it is alleged actual slavery has existed.

A government official declares hundreds of men and scores of women in other camps, abut which the secret service men are getting information, are held in slavery. The finding of seven dead bodies of Negroes in the Little Tennessee river led to the investigation. It is asserted the Negroes paid of their attempts to escape with their lives.

Camp No. 5 is situated thirty miles from Maryville and accessible only by a rough road over almost impassable mountains. The river and mountains make escape practically impossible. There until a week ago, according to the stories told to United Stated District Attorney Penland and the grand jury, 150 men were held as slaves.

Fearful lest the men indicted may learn the exact nature of the charges against them the official have placed witness. Jim Taylor, a Negro, said he had seen men beaten and kicked in the camp.

CHAPTER EIGHT
He Kept My Children

Department of Justice

Office of United States Attorney

Northern District of Mississippi- Clarkdale

Oxford, Miss

August 8th, 1921

The Attorney General

Washington, D.C.

Sir:

Herewith I hand you the facts as related to me by on Lucinda Holloman a Negro woman, who complains of one Mims

Wilson holds her child in peonage I know nothing of the facts except as detailed by her, and his matter is submitted by such action by the Department as may seem proper.

Respectfully

? E.

Department of Justice

Office of United State Attorney

Northern District of Mississippi-Clarkdale

Oxford, Miss, August 8th, 1921

In the matter of Mims Wilson

Alleged Violation of Section 5526 R.S. Holding Person to Peonage

Complainant----Lucinda Holloman a Negro woman apparently 36 or 37 years old.

Her family consist of; 1 daughter about 14 years old, named Mary Fraley and a son about 12 years old name Frank Fraley, both children by a former husband; and a baby boy about 1 year old. Her husband's name is Kicks Holloman.

In 1920, she lived on the plantation of Mr. William Lawler, Dublin, Coahoma County, Mississippi, where, with the aid of her two children she made a crop. About December she became dangerously ill, and Lawler sent to her to the home of a relative, Elnora Nathan, in Sunflower

County, for care and nursing. She stayed there awhile, end, not improving, was seat to a charity hospital at Jackson, Mississippi, and remained there until about March of this year.

When she went to Nathan's, she took with her, her bed-stand, chairs, trunk, cooking utensils, dishes, and clothes. She also took her children with her.

Elnora Nathan and her husband, Charlie Nathan, lived on this plantation of Mr. Mims Wilson, about six miles form Schalater, Sunflower County, Mississippi, where Charlie Nathan is a kind of foreman or superintendent on the plantation, and recording to the complainant " a mean negro

Mr. Wilson, the owner of the plantation is a middle-aged white man of family, residing in the town of Schlater.

When Complainant left the hospital in March, she went to Wilson's plantation to get her children. Charlie Nathan told her that she couldn't get them, that Mr. Wilson had fixed it so that she couldn't. She then went to see Mr. Wilson and refused and to let the children leave. She offered to pay him for feeding and having them cared for, but he said that she couldn't get money enough to pay him and that he rather have their labor on the plantation. She insisted that he tell her how much it would take to pay him for keeping the children, but could get nothing definite out of him, except that he refused to let her have the children. She then offered to farm a part of his land had done on Mr. Lawler's place, but he said that he had let out all of his land, and that he didn't have any of her to farm. Both the boy and girl worked for him last fall and this spring---the boy is a plow hand, and the girl hoed and help with the crops.

After she left Mr. Wilson place walked back to Schalter where she met Dr. Armour Fortwood a resident and practicing physician of Schlater and he offered to let her make a crop on his place and also agreed to pay Mr. Wilson the alleged debts of children if he would give them back to Complainant. But Mr. Wilson still refused to tell her what they owed him, saying that would rather have the children than the money because of their value as laborers on the plantation. He also objected to her staying near Schlater for the reason the children might and would likely run off and go to her. Mr. Wilson placed the children in the custody of his foreman, Charlie Nathan, who did not permit them to go off the place.

Complainant left Schlater walking toward Jackson. After reaching Inverness, some charitable people gave her enough money to pay her way to Jackson. While in Jackson she worked, and, with the help of her Church, managed to get enough money to pay her way to Oxford, having been referred by some of this office.

Complainant appears highly nervous and hysterical at times, but insists upon the truth of the facts as detailed above.

Respectfully submitted to the Department of Investigation, should it deem proper.

?

U.S. Attorney

CHAPTER NINE

EKO AND IKO CLYDE BEATTY CIRCUS SLAVES

Subject: Unknown Subjects:
            Eko and Iko Victims
            Involuntary Servitude

There are attached herewith copies of a letter dated July 25, 1946, at Walnut Grove, Illinois, furnished by Harry E. Friend. This letter was directed to our Chicago, Subject: Unknown Subjects:

Eko and Iko-Victims

Involuntary Servitude

There are attached herewith copies of a letter dated July 25, 1946, at Walnut Grove, Illinois, furnished by Harry E. Friend. This letter was directed to our Chicago, Illinois, office and contains the allegation that two Negroes are being held and mistreated by the " Clyde Beatty Circus".

I shall appreciate your advising me if any investigation of this matter is desired

Enclosure

Walnut Grove, Ill

July 25, 1946

FBI

Chicago, Ill

Dear Sirs:

"For giving this information it would cost me my life if it were known that I gave you such information, so you will treat it accordingly.

"The following I passed on to you as it was told to me by 2 persons commonly called Eko and Iko the so called sheep headed men of Clyde Beatty side show owned and operated by Pete Cur(?) 40 to 50 years age in some southern states there were born 2 albino Negros, as fair as any white man person with yellow colored hair kinky as any Negro, and at about the age of 6 and 7 these 2 Negro Boys were kidnapped by a Circus side show operator and were called sheep headed Boys because their hair resembled sheep wool, they were held and treated as slaves and some 20 years later Mother found them when a circus showed in a southern city where she lived, she took them from the circus. But their queer actions and money that was offered by same (or some) circus caused her let them go from her again. Later their own died and they were passed on to another operator and they are still virtually slaves today. I had the experience to travel with this same

sides how for 3 or 4 summers in Illinois and personally know of almost impossible conditions that they were forced to live under. There sleeping quarters while on location is or was a lousy show wagon, thousands of bed bugs in their beds possibly body lice. to have money they were forced to carry water and to do other show peoples flunky work, including show men's washing, and this money was used for clothing, etc.

"My understanding is that they were adopted to their present owner who is supposed to have paid certain money to their Mother while she lived, she is now deceased and what is being did now i dont know, but unless there is trust fund being set aside for them it is terrible, seems to me there present owner is as guilty of kidnapping as the original one that kidnapped these 2 colored Boys.

"Strange as it may seem, even though they were not gave

any schooling, they are good Christians and are able to play almost any musical instrument yet never had a lesson, and where you to ask how they account for this, their answer would be it was a gift as from God, and truly it must have been. Now they can neither read nor write yet I think they are good enough to be in Vaudeville and to easily earn their own living, and it should be made possible that they have their freedom. There could have been nothing nicer than for these 2 men to have been used as entertainers for our services men.

So I pass this information to you with the feeling that it warrants and investigation by FBI as from kidnapping standpoint.

"Then on this same show you will find Athelia the so called monkey girl living under almost impossible conditions the same as the 2 men Eko and Iko, Athelia is without brains cannot talk or understand any thing, must be over 50 years old, cannot control herself wears diapers, am I not right in passing this on to you, for some how it does not seem right that any person should be allowed to profit under such circumstances for there are too many ways to earn a decent living with using slaves saying nothing of kidnapping them.

"If the above is worth any thing. I am my family will gladly talk it over at anytime and give you still more actual facts about these folks.

"Am not writing you because of ill feeling, just that do not believe in such things and justice should prevail.

Your Truly

Harry E Friend

Friend's Grocery

CHAPTER TEN
MARY CHURCH TERRELL
JOURNALIST

CHAMBER OF COMMERCE

of Tampa Office of the Secretary

January 26, 1906

Dear Sir,

Your favor of January 20th, in which you express your regrets of being unable to accept the invitation of the Chamber of Commerce to attend the Immigration Convention to held here next month, has been received and noted. I regret your inability to be present.

Permit to say that one of the objects of the Immigration Convention is to denounce and take steps to counteract the damaging effect of the slander which have been circulated and given government endorsement in regard to the existence of peonage in the South. You, perhaps, are not fully sequainted with the extent of the misrepresentation to which the good people of the South, have been subjected though the agency of such writer s as Richard Barry and one Mary Church Terrill, a negro woman, who recently contributed to the Nineteenth Century Magazine as article full of the basest untruths; of such government agents as Mrs. Quackenbos, who, after a long series of investigations, in which trumped-up charges of peonage, were brought in our Federal Courts against employers of labor, has been unable to secure a single conviction. We of the South, and particularly of Florida deeply feel the injustice which has been permitted by the Department of Justice in the sending of such discredited sleuths among us and in the hounding down of innocent persons which has resulted in no case of which there was sufficient evidence to secure a conviction in a Federal Court A fair sample of the slanders which have been circulated is the statement of the negro woman above mentioned, who declares that white girls are worked side by side with negro convicts in our turpentine farms.—a statement utterly false. I regret exceedingly that you have evidently been influenced by such mendacious publications to reach the views you express in your valued letter. I feel certain that, if you understood more fully the facts, you would join with us in the effort to stop this wholesale flood of misrepresentation.

We are already preventing peonage, but, unfortunately, we have not been able to offset the misguided work of the Department of Justice or of the slanderers who have brought upon us to such undeserved censure. With expressions of the highest esteem, I am

Very respectfully yours.

Fred Thompson,
Secretary

CHAPTER ELEVEN

CHOCTAW INDIAN HELD IN PEONAGE

November 20, 1917

Joseph W. George, Esq.,
United States Attorney
Jackson, Mississippi

Sir:

In connection with the charges against S. Vance Posey in holding in peonage Tom Stephen, a full blood Choctaw Indian, there is enclosed herewith for your information a copy letter from the latter in regard to this matter.

> Respectfully
> For the Attorney General
> Assistant Attorney General
> Inclosure
> # 106804

Union, Miss, Nov. 16, 1917

Hon. Attorney General,

Washington, D.C.

Dear Sir:

On September 1, 1917 nearly three months ago, I wrote the Secretary of the Interior about the way I had been mistreated by Vance Posey and other men who live near Deemer, Miss., how I had been beaten, and defrauded and held in peonage there.

Under date of October 5, 1917, the assistant Commissioner of Indian Affairs wrote me that he taken the matter up with you, and I have heard no more about it.

If this means you have turned the matter over to the white men down here I know that won't do anything.

Perhaps Judge Niles, of Meridian, Miss., would if you sent it to him personally.

Vance Posey still hold our clothing and household goods clothing and bed clothing. Will you do anything about it?

Respectfully
Tom his (x) Stephen
mark

DEPARTMENT OF THE INTERIOR

OFFICE OF INDIAN AFFAIRS

WASHINGTON, D.C.

Sept 15, 1917

Land-Five Tribes

83262-17

In re-complaint of Tom Stephens

The Honorable The Secretary of the Interior

The Office has received a communication of September 1, 1917, purporting to the be signed by on, Tom Stephens (by mark) from Union, Mississippi, which communication contains a complaint concerning the treatment alleged to have been received by said Tom Stephen form S. Vance Posey and certain other persons in Mississippi. In said communication, it is claimed that Tom Stephens was a full blood Choctaw Indian identified by the Commission to the Five Civilized Tribe The name of To Stephen appears on the roll of identified Mississippi

Choctaw Indians opposite No. 2270, as a full blood Indian

Said identified Indian was, however, one of those who failed to comply with the provisions of Sections 41 to 44 inclusive, of the Act of Congress of July 1, 1902 (32 Stat. L, 641), in the matter of the removal and establishment of bon fide residence in the Choctaw Chicksaw country, Oklahoma, and therefore, failed of enrollment on the final rolls of the Choctaw Nation, and not being enrolled was not entitled to any distributive share of the Choctaw tribal land and funds. Its appears, however, from the above mentioned identification roll that he is full blood Choctaw Indian The complaint in the above mentioned letter of September 1, 1917, is to the effect that said Indian has been intimidated and defrauded and held in peonage If the facts alleged are true, they would appear to constitute violation of Section 269 of the penal laws of the United States as contained in the Act of Congress of March 4, 1909 (35 Stat. L. 1088-1142). The matter appearing to be one for investigation by the Department of Justice the Office recommends that said communication, purporting to the be that of said Tom Stephen, be forward to the Attorney General, with request that such action as the fact and the law may be found in warrant be taken therein.

CHAPTER TWELVE

PEONAGE IN THE FLORIDA, KEYS

E. T. Clyatt, of Jacksonville, Florida states that he was telephoned for while at Miami to take a position as foreman on Key Largo, and one to the Florida Keys.

J.C. Meredith, the constructing engineers, gave his orders to W.J. Krome, assistant, W. P. Dosenberry division engineer, J.R. Kerduff, resident engineer, and foreman Meredith, the constructing engineer, said there had been trouble with one of the foreman and that he wished Clyatt to help him out. Clyatt stated that after having had charge of the men on the island for about two month he became very disgusted with the conditions there, and the orders that he was asked to carry out, and he therefore gave up the position.

He stated that there was a general understanding from headquarters that no man should be allowed to leave the island, sick or well; that the men should be driven out of their tents at 5. A.M. each morning, and compelled to work whether they were in a condition to do so or not; that one of the commissary rules was that no man should receive and food if he did not work and that, as a result of this rule, many were ill with the fever and suffering from the treatment of bosses, where obliged to lie in their tents in a starving condition; that many died and more would have died had it not been for several negro women who had restaurants in or near the Keys and cooked for these men and gave them food. Clyatt states that the foreman and bossed lived in a house-boat which was situated at the landing on each island; that it was impossible for anyone to enter the island or leave it without walking over the house-boat; that when the company's boats landed with gangs of men.—and some four thousand men have been sent down there in the past year—they were slaves whether they owed the company money or not, for the reason that it was impossible for them to leave the island with Goode, Waldren, Hill, Ball, Grove and others.

That nearly all the New York men who came to the Keys were decoyed by the false representation of Employment Agent Sabbia in New York, and misreprenstations of Mr. Triay, Mr. Harley and Clemens, who had offices in Jacksonville and Miami. That many negroes where recruited from Georgia under false promises, and that when these workmen arrived on the Keys they were surprised to find that they were to work on the and island, having been told that they were to do railroad work on a few miles from Miami where they could go to town often.

That the natural conditions on the island were impossible. The water was put in tanks and carted on boats; that the men was obliged to sleep on the bare rocks; that the mosquitoes were poisonous and many became very ill of the insects and fever and lack of decent food. That in addition to this the bosses was brutal and beat the workmen often with axe handles, pointed revolvers at them and threatened them in every way if they seemed to ill to work rapidly. They many tried to get on the company's boats when get away when get away.

Clyatt states he himself had buried several and had to carry water while he was in almost dying conditions; that he say Anderson threatened by the foreman and beaten with a pick axe; that one W.C. Grover killed a man name Lindsay, a negro, at the same time he shot at Jake Anderson, and that the company kept Grover in their employ about six week after the shooting and later discharged him only, because Grover stole men from

the company and took them to Cape Stable, where he

received a bonus from another company. That in time Cylatt worked for a company he procured the release of some forty men, all of who owed a debt.

That he buried a negro who was found dead in his ten, having been refused food when he was sick; that one J.H. Staus, of Palm Beach, took him on his house boat and help Clyatt make a coffin for the many who had expired.

That a Mr. Herndon, walking boss for the company, had supervision of all the foreman and was kind to the men, and assisted Clyatt in releasing many against the company's orders.

Clyatt states that Schwartz sent about 800 to the Keys last year and Agent Sabbia about 4,000. That this agent is under contract with Meredith to supply a large number of men at time.

The East Coast Company operates every boat that runs between any of the islands camps and Miami or Key West. The workmen as thus at the mercy of the company, while on the islands, for no ships will take

Them on aboard with a pass until their debts to the

company are paid. These employed in the north are told they are wanted as iron workers, carpenters, bookkeepers, interpreters, masons, at $60.00 a month and are now forced to work with a pick and shovel.

One George Myer, manger of a fruit farm, five miles from Planter, Key Largo, has a small dock, and repeated request are made to him from distressed men to be permitted to go out on their pier and signal a passing vessels, but his orders were not to let anyone on the wharf who worked for the company. The men would sometimes hide in the bushes, and begging for assistance or pity. Some Negro cooks on the Keys have mercy upon them and give them food to take to the swamps, where they would hide until they might steal away on one of the boats belonging to the conch. These conch or fishermen owed small sail-boats and row-boats in those water, and would take men away from the islands, at night for $1.00 each, but when this was learned by the company's officials, the order came" shoot any fishermen who steals our men, just tell them that I will riddle their boats with bullets." Whether this was a warning or actually carried out, Mr. Clyatt did not state. My Clyatt states that there was convict camp at Ogus eleven miles from Miami, W.S. Hill being justice of the peace, and constables being L.M. Nicholson and man named Wilson, would arrest escaping peons on the pretense being a violation of the law to ride on a train with out money, they are forced back on the Key's to escape starvation.

In August 1905, at camp, some men tried to get away in a row-boat, having been refused a pass. After drifting around out in the sea without provisions and no drinking water, for two days, they drifted near Tug Pelton, the pilot of which quickly reported the same company and the launch was put out to capture the men. When the men were brought almost dying, boss Frozier kicked and ordered the men thrown overboard, but the were rescued by their companions.

If one man succeeded in leaving the island indebt to the commissary, the prices were immediately raised in order to make up the deficiency from the remaining workmen. Clyatt states that worked in the commissary and knows this if his own knowledge.

Many brought from New York was received in Savannah and Brunswick, Georgia, by Mr. Triay's agents in Jacksonville. Clyatt stated that he made several shipments coming from

Savannah and Sabbia, and that the order were that when the train left Savannah for Jacksonville the car in which the workmen were, was to be run down the track past the Jacksonville station and kept there while waiting for the Florida East Coast train; that in the way men were held in peonage before they every reached Miami or the islands; that many men were recruited also at East Palatka and Titusville, were the sheriff's and it fact all the sheriffs, on the East Coast of Florida are practically servants of the company, they arrest negroes, poor whites and escaping northern workmen on the Justice of peace, who sentenced to the chain-gang, when these men are them leased again to wok on the railroad or the surrounding turpentine camps. That many men are arrested several times in this way and forced to serve out, sentence or work out debts, before they finally make their actual escape.

W.S. Press carries mail from Miami to Plantation Key, and occasionally would pick up men who ask to be released and transport them to Miami to their freedom; that when this was learned by officials of the company, Press was instructed by the foreman not to bring out men who owed the company a bill.

That one Frank Gallst, and Italian jeweler in Miami assist Italians who have been under restraint at the keys and recently took the matter up with the Italia Consul at New York rising out of the arrest of one Angelo Seron, a decoyed Italian gentlemen who was decoyed to the Keys under promise of pay of $60. A month as interpreter, and who carried a note to that effect from Agent Sabbia address to Mr. Meredith. Arriving at the Keys he was given a pick and shovel and told to work. This he tried to, but being unaccustomed to hard labor he became ill. He then made his escape, but was arrested and put in the chain-gang, and through Mr. Gallst influence and the satisfying of the "charges against him, Seroni was released and sent to New York. His affidavit to hereto annexed. Jake Anderson says: I stayed at Key Largo eight months and begged to be sent out. Each time I was refused and beaten. I was shot through the arm by the foreman and did not receive any attention from the company after I was and did not receive any attention from the company after I was shot but was cared for and by one Mr. Dell and brought back to Miami.

I was kept on the Keys by force and not allowed on the

company's boats. After I was shot, I was forced to carry water for two days. When I finally go out I had to borrow money for my transportation.

(Signed) Jake Anderson

International Labor Defense

September 26, 1942

Wendell Berge

Assistant Attorney General

Department of Justice

Washington, D.C.

Dear Mr. Berge:

I am informed that a detail affidavit, charging one Cleo Young operator of a plantation near Timmonsville, South Carolina, with peonage has been filed with your department by David Williams, and escaped peon now resisting extradition proceedings in Union County, New Jersey.

The International Labor Defense, which as been assisting Mr. Williams in this efforts to remain in New Jersey and to resist extradition back to slavery, is deeply interested in the investigation and prosecution of the slavery conditions on the Young Plantation. I will appreciate it deeply if you will inform me what steps are taken by your Department to carry on this investigation.

It is in my understanding that Ms. Williams has children and grandchildren still on the Young Plantation, some of them at least held in the same condition of peonage as that from which he and his wife and part of his family escaped. It would be appear possible that and attempt at victimizing these members of Williams family may be made in retaliation for his exposure of the slavery condition in his affidavit to you, unless proper steps are taken by federal officials to safeguard them. Will you inform me what steps are possible, or have been taken, to this end? In connection with the prosecution for peonage and slavery violation of W.T. Cunningham, of Lexington, Georgia which has been going on at snail' s-pace since early 1940, you informed me on April 13 last, that "steps are now being taken looking toward the early presentation of the alleged violations to a grand jury in Georgia."

Will you please inform me of the progress, if any, of those steps, and whether the Department is still planning to prosecute them? As I told you in my communication of March 2 of this year, the delays of the Department in pressing this case and already at the time taken toll of several key witness, either by death, or though induction into the armed forces. Every further delay undoubtedly mitigates against successful prosecution of this outrageous flouting of our laws and Constitution.

It seems necessary to point out that peonage and the consequent morale-destruction is extremely harmful to the war-effort, nor that vigorous prosecution with a view to stamping out this practice is and essential part of the a win-the-war policy. Up to the present time, in the cases, which I have brought to your attention, and in numerous other cases which I am informed the Department has interested itself, action had been limited, apparently, to vague promises, and no vigorous prosecution has been forthcoming. It is to hope that the Department will undertake a more forthright policy of action in these matters.

Very sincerely

Vito Margantonio

CHAPTER THIRTEEN
PEONAGE CASES IN LOUISIANA

Department of Justice

Office of United State Attorney

Eastern District of Louisiana

New Orleans, LA. February 19. 1913

WRH-CWL

165796-1

The Attorney General,
Washington, D.C.

Sir:

As stated in the postscript to my letter of February 13, Mr. S.N. Allred, Special Agent of the Department reported to this office, and he was immediately furnished with the information we had relative to the alleged violations of the Peonage Law at Merryville, Louisiana and other points in Calcasieu parish. Mr. Allred was referred to Mr. Horace Wilkinson, of Port Allen, Louisiana, and also to at Mr. Covington Hall of Alexandria, Louisiana, who had made complaints to this office. Mr. Allred agreed to me a preliminary investigation at Baton Rouge, and obtains such information as he could at that point, and later to visit

Merryville, the place at which the law was alleged to have been violated. He returned to this office yesterday from Baton Rouge, and reported that he had interviewed Mr. Wilkinson and two particular Negroes who were said to have been employed at Merryville, Louisiana, and that from this investigation at Baton Rouge; he concluded that it would be useless for him to go to Merryville, Louisiana.

In view of the fact that the alleged violations of the law took place at Merryville, Louisiana, this office suggested to Mr. Allred that is investigation would not be completed unless he visited that point and interviewed the people there, particularly since Mr. Hall of Alexandria of this office that a Mr. J.W. Kelly, and certain other persons associated with him at Merryville, would be willing to aid and assist the Special Agent of the Department in obtaining all information possible, and Mr. Hall stated further that several ' raw cases" has happened in that town very recently. He stated that two men who were caught beating their way on the Santa Fe Railroad were sentenced by a justice of the peace to pay a fine of $3.00 each, and in default of payment, these men were taken in charge by the deputy sheriffs "belonging" to the American Lumber Company and forced to work out their fines at three days each in the mills of the company," and this in addition to these cases, Hall's friend, J.W. Kelly, would being a position to refer the Special Agent to a number of other cases.

We do not know whether Mr. Allred has changed his intention or not, but he stated to and attaché of this office last

Evening that on a receipt of a certain telegram, he was leaving New Orleans for some point in Alabama. We do not know whether it is his intention to consider this case closed or not. We are of the opinion, however, that the investigation should not be discontinued until after the operation of the sawmills at Merryville, and the conditions that have been thoroughly examined into. We believe that it was understood at the beginning that the investigation at Baton Rouge was only preliminary, and that the real should be made at Merryville, which is some 150 miles away, in the Southwestern part of the State.

Of course, we do not know what the facts might develop and as the jurisdiction of the case is the Western District, we felt that he had no authority to order Mr. Allred to go there, but we did advise him that in our opinion, the investigation should be continued.

Respectfully,

For the United States Attorney

Assistant United States Attorney

Matt Brisco A Negro in Bogalusa, Louisiana

The Attorney General,

Washington, D. C.

Sir:

Several weeks ago, complaints was made to me by one Matt Briscoe, a Negro, about the manner in which he had been treated and held in custody???? At Bogalusa. One cannot always rely on the accuracy of the statements of such complaints, but the facts, as stated by Briscoe, seem to show outrageously unjust treatment, and there is a possibility of the facts as stated by him justifying a prosecution under Section 19 of the Criminal Code, for conspiracy to deprive one of his liberty, guaranteed under the Constitution and laws of the United States. The prosecution, however, would not have been justified without evidence to substantiate the facts stated by Briscoe. I called in Special Agent Harris when Briscoe was here, and he had Mr. Harris take down the facts as Briscoe stated them, and requested Mr. Harris to make the investigation. I am interested in the successful prosecution of such cases and I know the Department is also, but it is useless to go into them without thorough preparation. Up to this time Mr. Harris had not investigated the case, or at least, he has not made any report of same to me. I am writing in the nature of complaint against Mr. Harris, because it may be the Department had kept him busy or other matters, such as violations of the Neutrality laws which he considers important, but which, to my mind, are not as important as such complaints as Briscoe's

Respectfully

Charlton Brattain

United States Attorney

Selling of Negro Family in Fluker, Louisiana

Indictments of Mississippi Case to be followed by Peonage Inquiry in Louisiana

By the Associated Press

NEW ORLEANS, Feb. 2, Department of Justice agents are investigating reports of Negro peonage in Louisiana. The indictment yesterday of Webb Bellue and John D. Alford of Amite County, Mississippi or charges of abduction, sale of

When they failed to find her according to the indictment enslavement of five Negroes will be followed by disclosure of peonage in St. Helena and Tangipahoa parishes in Louisiana. If evidence now in the hands of the United States Attorney here proves substantial, official said.

Alford and Webb were indicted on testimony that the had gone to the home of Crawford Allen, 50 years old Negro, near the Louisiana border in Amite County, Mississippi last August seeking his grown daughter.

they forced Allen to get out of a sick bed and accompany them on a farm in Fluker, Louisiana. The forced his wife and three children all under 12 year of age to accompany them.

The Negroes were taken at night. The family was sold for $20. The Department of Justice Agents charge. They were forced to work several weeks without pay and little food. An armed guard watched the Negroes.

Investigation if the case has revealed the existence of peonage conditions under which other Negroes are held in a stated of virtual enslavement officials said.

Adjunct Professor Clare Washington visit Fluker, Louisiana
Portland State University

A sharecropper's coin made by Kent of Fluker, Louisiana
This coin is called a brozine
Courtesy of Roy Curtis

CHAPTER FOURTEEN
WOMEN HELD IN PEONAGE

Gertha Haigs Beat With A Stick

Ethel Lee Davis Chain to A Bed

REPORT MADE BY: A.W. Davis

PLACE WHERE MADE Pensacola, Fla.

PERIOD FOR WHICH MADE Oct. 31, 1916

Title of case and offense charged or nature under investigation

In re Holloman and Williams "Referring to an alleged case of peonage"

On account of information received, and pursuant to instructions form the U.S. Attorney I went to Galliver, Fla., on Tuesday morning, Oct. 31st, and saw J.D. Kimbre, relative to the above, and made the following statement:

"On Tuesday evening, Oct 3rd, I was at Galliver depot when the East bound train come in. I saw a Negro woman with a baby in her arms attempt to board the train. A man slighted from the train and took hold of her preventing her from going aboard. She began pleading with the man, saying, "Please Mr. Williams let me go, I have got my ticket &c." The man, however, held her and conductor who had held the train pending the outcome of the dispute, gave me signal to go ahead. The man named

Williams told the woman to sit down, and when the westbound train came in shortly afterward, he took the woman aboard and they went away. I saw the man had a pistol but he did not draw it. While they were awaiting the arrival of the train I got into conversation with the woman, she stated she was to Moultire, Ga., and came to Holloman's still with a man who promised to marry her if she went with him, he however had failed to marry her. She had been worked enough in the ten months to pay that. She had cord wood and dipped gum, they had beaten her once and threatened to kill her. "She was afraid of them and wished the sheriff would take her, altho she had done nothing, but she would rather work for the county than go back Holloman's still."

AllenT. Carr Station Agent at Galliver, corroborated the above statement. I then went to Holloman's still about twenty-five miles in the woods and interviewed the woman Gertha Haigs whose statement in substance was as follows:

" I came here from Moultrie, Ga., on January 1st, of this year with Doc Tate and Cleveland Holt, the latter promised to marry me if I would go with him, but wanted to go home but I was told I would have to work out the price of the railroad ticket upon which I cam here. I have worked from that time until now, and I was sure I had worked along enough to pay for the ticket. Mr. Holloman told he did not want me to go away until Cleveland Holt had paid up what he owed him, as he knew he would not stay if I went away. I told him I would not, but I wanted to go home to my children which I had left in Moultrie. In the beginning of October my mother wrote me that she had sent me ticket to come home, so I walked to Holts and got my ticket, and then went to Galliver to wait for the train.

I had my baby with me. When the train came in, I was about to go aboard when Mr. Williams jumped off and grabbed me, and held me so I couldn't get on. I begged him to let me go, but he held on, and told the conductor to go on, as he had a warrant for me as I had stolen some money. I asked him to show me the warrant, but he said the sheriff would be there shortly. When the westbound train came Holloman who had been looking for me then came aboard. We got off at Harrell and Mr. Holloman and

Mr. Williams made me get into Mr. Holloman's car, which was at the station, when we started back for the still. "You told me a dam lie didn't you" (this referred to my promise not to go away). I said "Yes Sir", he said " I don't know sir." He then stopped the car and put out the lights. Mr. Williams go out and cut a stick and gave it to Mr. Holloman, who whipped me with it, after he has whipped me he said, " Now you better keep you damned mouth shut or I will do you worse." He said he was going to keep me here until Cleveland pays up what he owes him. Mr. Williams had whipped me sometime before this with a rope."

I was told that Mr. Holloman while looking for Gertha Haigs at Holt asked a woman named Gertha Holt, if she had seen anything for the Haigs woman. This woman is located at Clarey, near Crestview. Mr. Vickery was in charge of the train, which the woman was trying to board.

Copy Chief Bielaske

Washington, D.C. United States Attorney

Outline of Testimony

Testimony of Cleveland Holts.

He testified that after the first beating of Gertha Haigs , by Williams he saw Mr. Holloman by the commissary and Holloman stated to him, he could leave if dissatisfied, upon payment of the debt, but that if he left without paying the debt, that he, Holloman, " would get him." That he understood that to be that Holloman would whip him, as he had whipped the other, or would put him on the chain-gang, as he had done others.

Testimony of Charlie Bronson

Bronson stated that he was working for Holloman that he was indebted to him and left. That prior to his leaving, they said they " would get him," if he left. After he left, they had him arrested for carrying concealed weapons and living in adultery with some woman, and he put on the hard road for 6 month for carrying concealed weapons and the Grand Jury of the State refused to indict him of adultery. That afterward, having served 6 month, he went to the place of a man named Joyner and secured employment and Joyner to pay his account with Holloman. He stated that he went with Joyner to Holloman's to get his furniture and while there in the commissary. Atwell and Williams assaulted him with a stick and severely beat him. The records of the County Judge show both these prosecutions and a plea of guilty by Bronson to carrying concealed weapons and the binding over of Bronson to the Grand Jury for adultery. It also shows the entry of a plea of guilty by Atwell and Williams for assaulting C. Bronson.

Testimony of Kimbro

See report of Special Agent

Testimony of Vickery.

Captain Vickery, conductor of the L. & N. R.R. Co., corroborated the statement made by the woman as the Williams preventing her from boarding the train on the night in question, and that Williams and Holloman boarded that train at one station, rode to the next depot, got off, and Williams again boarded the train and rode to Galliver, at which place he got off and prevented the woman from boarding the train one station. rode the next depot, got off, and Williams again boarded the train and rode to Galliver, at which place he got off and prevented and woman from boarding the train.

Testimony of Miller and Demarcus.

Flagman Miller and Demarcus, the train butcher, also corroborate the story.

Department of Justice
UNITED STATE ATTORNEY
Northern District of Mississippi
Clarkdale, Mississippi
50-679

September 10, 1937

The Attorney General

Department of Justice

Washington, D.C.

In re: United States vs. J.S. Decker, Peonage

Reference in made to your letter dated September 1, 1937, requesting report concerning the arrest of one J.S. Decker on a charge of peonage, and accordingly I submit below a detailed statement of the case.

Early in July both the Sheriff and District Attorney of Tallahatchie County, Mississippi reported to writer an alleged violation of the Federal peonage laws on the part of

J.S. Decker , and based on these reports I promptly referred the matter to the Federal Bureau for appropriate investigative attention.

   The investigation conducted by the Bureau has been completed and reflects a very aggravated offense. According to investigation Harry H. Dogan Sheriff of Tallahatchie County received a complaint on July 10, 1937, from a Negro J.W. Wiggins , who came to the sheriff's office telling a story about his wife being chained up in a cabin on the J. S. Decker farm. The sheriff, with one of his deputies, proceeded to Decker's farm and upon arrival went forthwith to Decker's house, and when Decker came to the door he had a revolver in his belt; the sheriff ordered Decker to put away his gun

and to show him into the cabin in which Wiggin's wife was being held. According to the sheriff, when he entered the cabin, the negro woman, Ethel Lee Davis (alleged common law wife of J.W. Wiggins" was fastened by a trace chain, one end of which was looped around her neck and fastened by a padlock connected to two links of the chain, the other end of the chain being secured to a bed in the cabin. The Sheriff ordered Decker to release the woman, which Decker did, unlocking the padlock with a key, which he had in his pocket.

Mr. Dogan stated that on asking Decker why he had done such a thing Decker replied, " the s—o—b—are running away on me and I'm getting G—d—tired of it." The sheriff then took Ethel Lee Davis to Sumner, Mississippi, and she was Wiggins were left there.

Mary Doyle, negro, grandmother of Ethel Lee Davis advised that Ethel Lee Davis and J.W. Wiggins had come to her home on July 4, 1937, and that a short while after arrival there Decker came to her home and forced Ethel Lee Davis and J. W. Wiggins to accompany him at the point of a gun.

Ethel Lee Davis stated that she went to work on Decker place near the end of 1936, drawing $15.00 at Christmas time and beginning March 1, 1937, drew @12.00 each month until July. This money was given to J.W. Wiggins and Ethel Lee Davis jointly. She stated that Decker worked her too hard, and she became ill with attacks of asthma and wanted to leave; that J.W. Wiggins mention to Mr. Decker that they were going to leave, and that on July 3rd she and Wiggins left the Decker farm going to her grandmother's home at Tutwiler, Mississippi; that shortly after arriving there Decker came to the house and waked them up with the point of a pistol carried them in his truck back to his farm.

When they arrived at the farm they were both chained to trees for about two hours, and Mr. Decker carried them chained up in his car to Joe Hyde to see if he would pay the debt, which the two Negroes owed him. Decker claimed that the negroes owed him $176.00 in reply which Hyde stated that was pretty high for five months furnish and made inquiry as to whether or not the negroes were allowed anything for the crops which they had made, in reply to which Decker answered, "Hell, no. I am not allowing them nothing for the crop."

Ethel Lee Davis stated that Mr. Hyde declined to pay the debt because it was too much; that they were then taken back to the Decker farm, and on the following day the two of them, Ethel Lee Davis and J. W. Wiggins, left again, going to the house of a friend; shortly after arriving there Decker came to the house, but Wiggins made his get-away.

CHAPTER FOURTEEN

FEDERAL BUREAU OF INVESTIGATION

FILE NO. 50-331

REPORTED MADE BY   WILLIAMS R.
JENKINS WRJ:PES

TITLE   JEFF LITTLE

DATE: 6-4-45

REPORT MADE AT   NEW ORLEANS, LA

SYNOPSIS OF FACTS:

Edward Earl Williams, negro, age 62, claims to have held against his will on subject's farm by threats of subject to kill him if he left. Also claims that he was forced to remain on farm since subject claimed Williams owed him $40.00 house rent. Williams left subject's farm by means of collection taken up among Negroes in the community and given to Williams so that he could report his situation to the "law."

DETAILS

This case is predicated upon information furnished by the victims, Edward Earl Williams 1319 Arabella Street, New Orleans, Louisiana, who came to this office on May 14, 1945, and furnished the following information:

Williams stated that sometimes during the last week of December 1944, he went to the farm of Jeff Little, Rockport, Mississippi and asked for a job. Little told Williams that he would give him a job and agreed to pay him $1.00 per day and keep. Williams stated that he told Little he was preacher and due his age could only perform garden work. Williams stated he worked in Mr. Little's yard for three or four days and then Little made him go out into the field and plow. Williams said

he plowed for about three week and stated that Little never paid him but 50 cent per day. Williams stated that each time Little paid him at the rate of 50 cent per day he asked him for the other money, but Little would

always stall him off and tell Williams he did not have the money Williams advised that when he moved to the Little farm he was allowed to move into a small house. About March or April, 1945, Little told Williams that he would have to move from this house because he was going to use this house for some else. Williams told Little that he didn't want to use this house for someone else. Williams told Little that he did not want to move because the house to which he was move had no glass windows. Little told Williams that him that if he left his farm he would charge him $10.00 per month for the months which Williams had lived in the first house. Williams told Little that he could not pay this since Mr. Little had never paid him more than 50 cent a day.

Williams stated that the night after this occurrence he went to the home of Ed Robinson Negro preacher in New Hebron, Mississippi The following morning Little came to Robinson's house and told Williams that he would have to pay the $40.00 due rent or return to his farm and work out the $40.00. Williams then moved back to Little's farm and moved into the house which Little had designated for him to move into.

Williams stated that about the middle of April, 1945,

Little came to the field with his son, Joe Little, Little told Williams that some of the other Negroes on Joe Little's farm were claiming that Williams was putting the hoodoo on them. Little told Williams that he was going to kill him if he didn't stop putting the hoodoo on the other Negroes.

Williams said that one Sunday about the middle of April 1945, a group of Negroes came to the farm and asked Williams to preach a burial sermon. He stated that the Negroes gave him $3.00 to preach the burial sermon but that Mr. Little found out about it and made him give the $3.00 back. Little told Williams that he could not go to preach the burial service and also told the group of Negroes to stay away from the farm and to leave Williams alone.

Williams stated the Ed Robinson the negro preacher New Hebron, Mississippi, later told him that Little went to his house and told him to stay away from Williams and to not allow Williams to come to his house anymore. Williams stated that a few days later Little again came out to the field where he was working and accused him of always being gone preaching when she should be at home working. Williams stated that Little then slapped him, he slap knocked him down, after which Little kicked him. At this time Little told him that if he ran off

Again he would have the "law bring him back and they would kill. Little also told him at that time that he had better not tell anyone about the slapping or kicking, because he would kill him. Williams also quoted Little as saying that *"we now have a different president in the White House so we get some Negroes and make them stay on the farm and work."*

Williams stated after this last occurrence he stayed on the Little farm for about three weeks because he was afraid to leave. He said that the Negroes in Rockport, Mississippi learned of his situation and took up a collection to that Williams could leave and report his situation to the "law Williams said he left Mississippi and did not report it to the Mississippi " law" as he was afraid that they would take him back to Mr. Little. Williams said he went from Rockport,

Mississippi, to Jackson, Mississippi, and then came by bus to New Orleans, Louisiana inasmuch as he wanted to report his situation to the "law in New Orleans because

New Orleans was his old home.

Williams stated that he intended to remain in New Orleans and would either be at the address of 1310 Arabella Street or the person at this address would know his whereabouts.

It would be noted that Williams was crying throughout this interview and it was extremely difficult to secure a coherent story from him. Williams described the subject Jeff Little as follows:

Age	about 70
Race	white
Height	6'
Weight	160 pounds
Hair	gray
Eyes	wears glasses
Build	tall and slender
Occupation	farmer
Residence	Rockport, Mississippi

The following physical description of the victim Edward Earl Williams was secured by interrogation and observation:

Age	62
Date of birth	December 1, 1882
Place of birth	Mobile, Alabama
Race	Negro
Hair	black and gray
Height	5'2
Weight	120 pounds
Eyes	blue
Build	small
Occupation	preacher farm laborer
Relatives	brother: Jim William, 4717 Chestnut Street, N.O.L.A

This case is being considered referred upon completion to this office origin. Jackson has been designated office of origin inasmuch as any investigation authorized by the Bureau will take place in the Jackson Division.

Copy

New Orleans, LA., August 25, 1913

Hon. W. H. Osborn,

Commissioner of Internal Revenue,

Washington, D.C.

Sir:

Referring to your letter of July 23, 1913, I beg to state that complaint made by Joe Herring at Elaine, Ark was turned over to General Dy. Collector W.H. Elstner for investigation. I am this day in receipt of his report as follows:

"I have to report that the 20th inst. I visited Elaine, Ark and endeavored to find Joe Herring to investigate statements made in his letter to the District Attorney at Oxford, Miss. I was unable to find him.

On the 22nd inst., in company with Division Dy., Collector W.G. Comings, of the District of Ala., I visited the plantation of Jerry Robinson, Swan Lake., and saw Rosie Herring. She state that wanted to leave but had to stay until she got out of debt; that she had never received a full settlement for last year's crop; that did not get enough to ear or wear; that ration was issued for two weeks at a time, consisting of a little bacon, flour and meal; that the only way she could leave was to run away, and she was afraid to do this, for if they caught her they would bring her back and whip her and put her back to work; that they whipped Joe Herring because Joe Robinson intercepted a letter he has written to Washington telling of conditions on this place; that he was also whipped because he did not force her into the field one day and objected to them whipping her.

Joe Fleming , who says he is from Rapides Parish La.. state that he and his father and family wanted to leave but cannot on account of an alleged debt; that, Willie Mathis and Calvin Hodges ran away ,and that he and Hodges were followed and caught near Tutwiler, Miss., and brought back and put to work; that it is a common thing for Jerry Robinson to whop the hands in the field' that he stripes the body and uses a strap; that Effie Page ran off and was followed ran off and was followed and caught near Jackson and brought back by J.F. Garnes, the overseer that it is well known on this plantation that you cannot leave until you are out of debt, and if you do that you will be brought back and whipped; also that statements of what you owe are rare things.

Rob Mathis , old negro from Arkansas who had been on this place for 11 years, states about the same. He says that he had no settlement for last year's crop; that he does not even know what they charge him for his clothes or food; that he knows he cannot leave until he pays out; He told me that, if he was in some place where he could stay away, he could and would tell thing of interest, but they he was afraid of being seen talking to us, for it they found that he told me anything they would kill him.

Copy of Burgh's letter -2-

In reference to the sale of liquors we found that Grant Kelly was selling, but for the reason that we has succeeded in talking to the above-named parties without the knowledge of Jerry Robinson or J.F. Carnes, the overseer we left this matter for another time; to have pressed it now would have got these negroes into trouble and would have complicated the investigation as to peonage if one should be made. Kelly, from what I can learn, is selling liquor with full knowledge of Robinson and the overseer.

Any one can see for talking to these Negroes that their condition is bad. They are in mortal dread of being seen talking to any one, and I believe they are telling the truth about peonage being practiced on this place. The plantation is situated away down on the river, and the owner could do almost anything and one be wiser.

It is my opinion that, if an investigation is made by the Department of Justice, conditions will be found as stated by Joe Herring if such investigation he made I will gladly give officer information as the location of the these cabins and how to get in there without making inquiries.

The foregoing report is respectfully submitted for your consideration. I return herewith copy of communication from Joe Herring enclosed in your letter above referred to.

> Respectfully
>
> (Signed) H. B. Burch,
>
> Revenue Agent

Copy

April the 8th, 1912

To the Civil Government of the United States

Gentlemen:

We poor colored men here in the State of Mississippi and poor women does ask the Civil Government to please please sen us some one here to take us out of this place our wives and children are naked and barefooted and were are the same they have here what is know as "pennick slavery" they go to work and beat poor negroes with sticks and shoot them and kill them just like they were Wild Bears in the Woods and we make big crops here and the Wont settle with us they jus work us like dogs and mules and just take our labor if you think we are lieing please send your men here and Just let them See our little Naked Children and wives and come question the Labor on the place. When you send some one please send them to carry us away if you dont they will Shoot us down after they are gone, please Come and take us away from here Give us half enough to eat. These men is Jerry Robinson, and Harry Seaton Robinson, Albin, Miss. And all down to Swan Lake and had people whipping with straps wight about 6 pounds they whip us to work by the day and don't pay for that they don't pay for nothing and wont furnish clothes.

We are just forced some complaint to ask for Help and if the Civil law dont help we are Bound to die for the Need of Help through written and signed by Sam Dromond and Jake Hicks and Harry Henry and Joe Herring and Joe Roundtree and Wil Smith and Joe Carson and Jerry Weekly.

Department of Justice

Office of United State Attorney

Northern District of Mississippi

February 20, 1912

The Attorney General

Washington, D. C.

Sir:

Replying to yours or the 16th inst., inclosing copy of a letter from A.N. Edens, of Grapeland, Texas, with reference to alleged condition of peonage practiced by C.L. Townes and others, of Glendora, Miss., beg to say that I will investigate matter as best I can with the means at my command, and report to the Department.

Respectfully

William D. Frazier

U.S.

TERMS OF COURT.

EASTERN DIVISION:
At Aberdeen—First Mondays of April and October.

WESTERN DIVISION:
At Oxford—First Mondays of June and December.

Department of Justice.

Office of United States Attorney,   CWL-CES

NORTHERN DISTRICT OF MISSISSIPPI,

OXFORD.

160502-2
WRH-CWL

February 20, 1912.

The Attorney General,

     Washington, D. C.

Sir:

     Replying to yours of the 16th inst., inclosing copy of a letter from A. N. Edens, of Grapeland, Texas, with reference to alleged condition of peonage practiced by C. L. Townes and others, of Glendora, Miss., beg to say that I will investigate the matter as best I can with the means at my command, and report to the Department.

     Respectfully,

               William D. Frazee

             U. S. Attorney.

160502-4

Black Bayou in in Tallahatchie County

Grain in Swan Lake, Mississippi

WEBB, MISSISSIPPI

DEPARTMENT OF JUSTICE

UNITED STATES ATTORNEY

NORTHERN DISTRICT OF MISSISSIPPI

Clarkdale, Mississippi

July 28, 1926

The Attorney General,

Washington, D.C..

Sir:-

I am enclosing herewith for your inspection report of special agents of the Department upon and alleged violation of Section 269 C.C., peonage.

I am of the opinion that the person under investigation should be prosecuted on a charge of peonage, and expect to present the matter to the grand jury at our next regular term of court in October.

I will note that Taylor Collins and George Walker,negroes are now confined on the county farm in Bolivar county serving a sentence of one year for violation of Section 875 Hemmingway's Mississippi Code which section has been held to be unconstitutional.

You will also note the copy of the attached affidavit does not seem to charge any offense, and there is no question by what thesed convicts are being held on a void conviction. However, I do not see that the United States Attorney has any authority to institute proceedings to have the negroes released, unless we can proceed on the grounds that they are material government witnesses.

Please advise me if, in your opinion, it will be proper for me to proceed, privately or as United States Attorney to institute babeas corpus proceedings to have these prisoners released so that I may hold them as witnesses for the government.

Respectfully

John R. Cook
United States Attorney

UNITED STATES ATTORNEY

NORTHERN DISTRICT OF MISSISSIPPI

Clarksdale, Mississippi,
July 28, 1926.

The Attorney General,
Washington, D. C.,

Sir:-

I am enclosing herewith for your inspection
report of special agents of the Department upon
an alleged violation of Section 269 C. C., peonage.

I am of the opinion that the persons under
investigation should be prosecuted on a charge of
peonage, and expect to present the matter to the
grand jury at our next regular term of court in
October.

You will note that Taylor Collins and George
Walker, negroes are now confined on the county
farm in Bolivar county serving a sentence of one
year for violation of Section 875 Hemmingway's
Mississippi Code, which section has been held to be
unconstitutional. You will also note the copy
of the attached affidavit does not seem to charge
any offense, and there is no question but what
these convicts are being held on a void conviction.
However, I do not see that the United States Attorney
has any authority to institute proceedings to have
the negroes released, unless we can proceed on the
grounds that they are material government witnesses.

Please advise me if, in your opinion, it will
be proper for me to proceed, privately or as United
States Attorney, to institute habeas corpus proceedings to have these prisoners released so that
I may hold them as witnesses for the government.

Respectfully,

John H. Cook,
United States Attorney. 50-40-2-1

JHC:VC
encl 3

175

Copy

Jackson, Miss.

Dec. 30, 1912

Mr. R. C. Lee,

Destrect Reurner,

I will write you stating you what trouble I am in. I am away from home and afraid to go back. And want you to please send and get my family at Pelshatchie, Rankin County, Miss Get off the train at Pelahatchie, ten miles South of Pelshatchie. I have been working on this det leven years, and every year it amounts up to more, and I am sick and hardly able to work, and now I ask you for help. This year amounts up to $780.05. I Charley Smith live at R.E. Patrick. He has been whipping me and my family for years, and I could not open my mouth, and I see I Cant no pay the det he claims I owe, and now I am not able to do much work, and I thought I would write and explain it to you. I has a wife and eight children.

Huntsville, Alabama

August 26, 1973

United States District Attorney,

Jackson, Mississippi

PEONAGE/Clarksdale, Miss

Dear Sir:

I note a newspaper account from Clarkdale Miss, dated August 25, 1937 where one J.S. Deckerhad been arrested for peonage, I know nothing about this case, but I think I know something of conditions that did exist in the delta country during the year of 1921-22.

I resigned as Deputy United States Marshal, for the Northern District of Alabama, March 1921 to except a place as Assistant Special Agent for the Y & M. V. RR.Co. with headguarters at Greenwood, Miss I had about three hundred miles to look after a Detective for the said railroad, I met a conditino that I dnot think existed anywhere in the United States, the negro share cropper in my opinion and obsevation, was just as much in bondage as they was before the war between the states.

I am setting in the Mayors office one morning in Greenwood, Miss, when a man marched a trembling Negro in the said " Mayor I want you to send this Negro to the penitentiary, he was running away, I caught him, he got goods from me under false pretence, so send him off, as he was trying to run away and I caught him, then the Negro put up a pitify cry to get this boos-man to not send him off, but to pay his fine for him, he would go back home, work for the boss-men the rest of his life, if he would not send him off, the boss-man cursed hin, told him he was only trying to get away, but the Negro assured hie would never do it again, so the boss-man asked the mayor how much he would fine this Negro, the mayor said $50.00 and cost, then the boss-man said " I will pay it, go on back, if you try to run away again I will kill you " after the Negro had gone, the boss-man asked the mayor bow much the cost ws, and paid the cost, but not the fine, I do not know whether the negro ahd the fine to pay or not, by my opinon is he did pay it.

I saw other things, which convinced me, they kept the negroes in slavery.

I am a democrat, was born and reared in North Alabama, I ans no negro lover, I think every men should have that which is right and just. I know the Miss, Delta Negros did not get it while I was there.

You may know more about the conditions there now than I do, but I knew it then.

Blind copy for Assistant Attorney General

Washington, D.C.

NATIONAL ASSOCIATION FOR THE ADVANCEMENT OF COLORED PEOPLE

March 4, 1927

Hon. John G. Sargent, Attorney General
Department of Justice
Washington, D.C.

Dear Sir:

We are in receipt of a letter charging peonage practices on a plantation in Mississippi, the nearest town to which according to our correspondent, is Minoler, Mississippi.

The letter states that on this plantation two hundred or more colored people are being held by the owner of this plantation, Charlie Johnson, by name; and that both men and women are driven, whipped and stripped.

I am referring this matter to you for such action as you feel the matter warrants.

Very truly yours,
James Weldon Johnson
Secretary

NATIONAL ASSOCIATION FOR THE
ADVANCEMENT OF COLORED PEOPLE
69 FIFTH AVENUE, NEW YORK
(AT FOURTEENTH STREET)

TELEPHONE STUYVESANT 6548

JAMES WELDON JOHNSON,
SECRETARY
WALTER WHITE,
ASSISTANT SECRETARY

March 4, 1927

Hon. John G. Sargent, Attorney General
Department of Justice
Washington, D. C.

Dear Sir:

We are in receipt of a letter charging peonage
practices on a plantation in Mississippi, the nearest
town to which, according to our correspondent, is
Winoler, Mississippi.

The letter states that on this plantation two
hundred or more colored people are being held by the
owner of this plantation, Charlie Johnson, by name; and
that both men and women are driven, whipped and stripped.

I am referring this matter to you for such
action as you feel the matter warrants.

Very truly yours,

Secretary

JWJ/RR

50 - 40 - 4 - 1

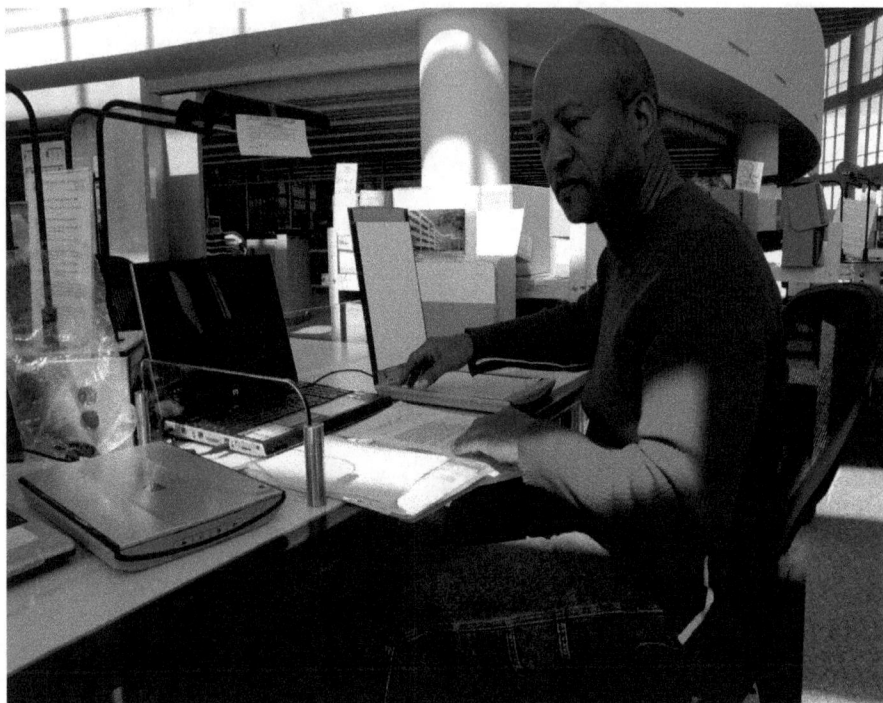

Walter C. Black, Sr., conducting peonage research at the National
Archives in College Park

Antoinette Harrell conducting Peonage Research at the National
Archives.

Antoinette Harrell conducing peonage research in Amite County, Mississippi

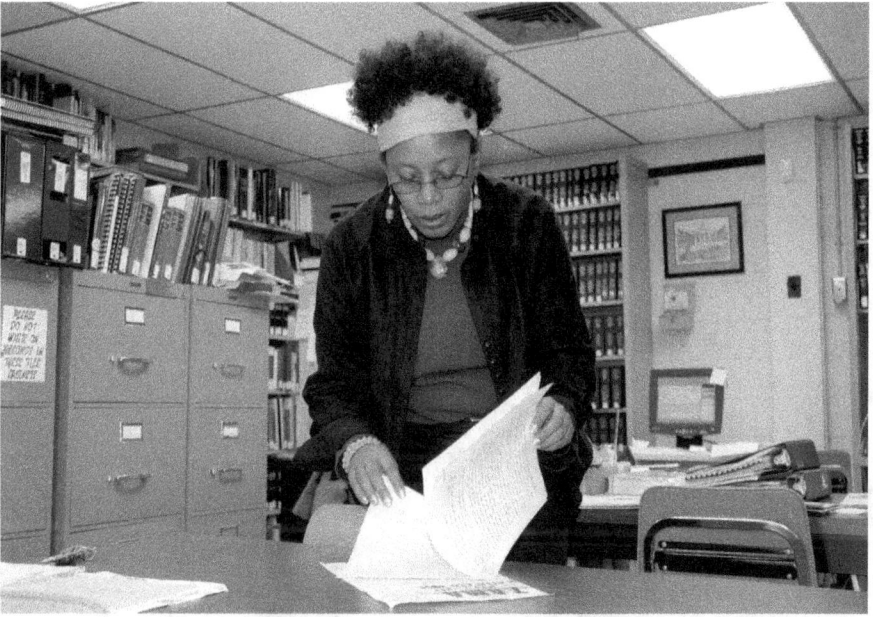

Antoinette Harrell looking at timber records at the Attala County
Public Library. Justice of Peace and Sheriff records in the attic in Attala
County

Top Photo: The late Dr. Ron Walters, Professor Rebecca Hensley on a Poverty Tour
Bottom Photo: Home in Webb, Mississippi

Homes in the Mississippi Delta

Selected Bibliography

NATIONAL ARCHIVES, WASHINGTON, D.C.
Record Group 60: General Records of the Department of Justice, 1790-1989

PHOTOGRAPHS
WALTER C. BLACK, SR.

EKO AND IKO PHOTOGRAPH POST CARD
Hake's Americana & Collectibles
Page 103

UNITED STATES PRESIDENTS
From Wikipedia, the free encyclopedia Images
Page 46 Franklin D. Roosevelt
Page 47 Warren G . Harding
Page 48 Calvin Coolidge

SPECIAL THANKS

The National Archives
Amite County Courthouse
Attala County Courthouse
Town of Glendora, Mississippi
Town of Webb, Mississippi
Professor Clare Washington
Portland State University

Contact the Author
Antoinette Harrell
Nurturing Our Roots Blog Talk Radio
http://www. blogtalkradio.com/antoinette-harrell
afrigenah@yahoo.com
504.858.4658

Index